Favourite

in

Devon

with local authors and walkers

edited by

Simone Stanbrook-Byrne

and

James Clancy

CULM VALLEY PUBLISHING

Published by:
Culm Valley Publishing Ltd
Culmcott House
Mill Street, Uffculme
Cullompton, Devon
EX15 3AT, UK
Tel: +44(0)1884 849085
E-mail: info@culmvalleypublishing.co.uk
Website: www.culmvalleypublishing.co.uk

First published 2013

ISBN 978-1-907942-10-5 paperback

British Library Cataloguing-in-Publication Data
A catalogue record for this book is available from the British Library

Typeset by Culm Valley Publishing Ltd
Printed and bound by TJ International Ltd, Padstow, Cornwall

Front cover image: Valley of Rocks (Walk 16)
Back cover image: Lone Pine, Raddon Hills (Walk 4)

Contents

Foreword

In this neat volume of circular walks in Devon, Simone Stanbrook-Byrne and James Clancy have persuaded some of the county's most respected walkers and authors to divulge secrets of their favourite routes. A quick scan of the contents gives a sense of the variation of terrain covered – readers are invited to follow paths through the rolling Blackdown Hills, along the rugged North Devon coast, across wildest Dartmoor and beside the curling River Dart.

In each of these chapters it is the connection to, and familiarity with, a well-trodden path that shines through: from Adam Hart-Davis' carefully observed line drawings of structures around the River Erme, to Simon Dell's informed eye spotting vermin traps and pillow mounds underfoot (which otherwise might have passed unnoticed).

For me it is the writer's familiarity with a route – through the years or across the seasons – that marks this book as special. I learn where rivers rage in winter, where kingcups glow in summer and where starlings wheel in autumn skies.

There is drama too in the scenery encountered: I can feel the wind buffeting as an astonishing view at Morte Point is revealed, and the thrill of stumbling across an ancient stone row on Dartmoor.

But what's the use of a book of walks if it a) doesn't fit in your pocket, b) give very clear directions and a readable map, c) list where to get a cup of tea? This book does all this exceptionally well, and it identifies the length and level of the walks, places of interest, loos, public transport and places to stay.

Walk on!

Jane Fitzgerald
Editor, Devon Life, to May 2013

Introduction

On any walk common sense must prevail: be properly shod and take care where you put your feet, be prepared for any kind of weather, take food and first aid supplies with you and make sure someone knows where you're going. Mobile phones are often useless in the middle of nowhere.

We feel it's important that you take the **correct OS map** with you plus a **compass** (where advised) and are conversant with their use. Our sketch maps are precisely that – sketches – and are for rough guidance only and not necessarily to scale.

You know you've had a good day's walking when you get home safely at the end of it.

Follow the countryside code:
www.naturalengland.org.uk/ourwork/enjoying/countrysidecode/def ault.aspx

Dartmoor foal (Walk 11)

Disclaimer

Points that should be borne in mind on any route:

Public footpaths can be legally re-routed from the path shown on the map. In such cases they are usually clearly signposted.

Most public footpaths are on private land. Please respect this.

Don't be surprised to find livestock grazing on public footpaths – and treat all animals with caution and respect.

If a field is planted with crops across a footpath, provision is usually made around the edge of the field.

Landmarks can change: trees and hedges may disappear; streams can dry up in warm weather or flood after heavy rain; stiles turn into gates and vice versa; fences appear where previously there was no boundary. Even views are different as the seasons progress. In such cases a modicum of common sense must be exercised – in conjunction with the OS map.

Public footpaths are at times blocked by barbed wire etc. Should this render the route impassable find the shortest detour around that section.

Please leave gates as you find them and if you have to climb them do so at the hinge end where it's stronger.

Exercise caution on wet stiles – they can be extremely slippery.

Take all your rubbish with you, please don't damage anything during the walk and please don't pick plants.

Please keep your dogs under proper control.

We hope that you enjoy these walks without mishap, but urge you to exercise common sense at all times. Neither the authors nor Culm Valley Publishing Ltd accepts responsibility for any misadventure that may occur during, or arise from, these walks and suggested routes.

Walk Locations

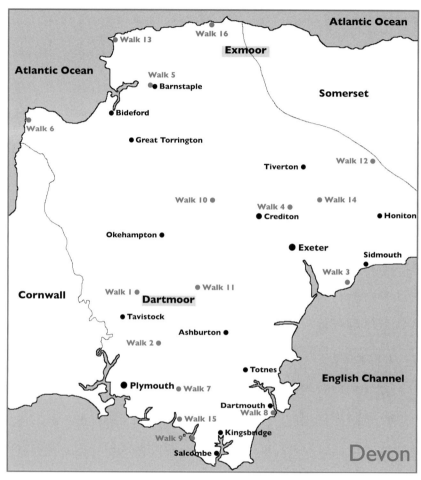

Walk 1	Horndon	Walk 9	Bantham/Thurlestone & Avon
Walk 2	Ditsworthy Warren/War Horse	Walk 10	Zeal Monachorum
Walk 3	Otterton & the River Otter	Walk 11	Bennett's Cross/Grimspound
Walk 4	Thorverton & Raddon Hills	Walk 12	Hemyock
Walk 5	Barnstaple	Walk 13	Mortehoe & Lee
Walk 6	Exploring the Hartland Penins.	Walk 14	Bradninch
Walk 7	Above & Beside the River Erme	Walk 15	Kingston & Wonwell
Walk 8	Exploring Around the Dart	Walk 16	Little Switzerland

Walk 1

Horndon

by **Sue Viccars**

Distance: 4¼ miles / 6.8km

The great granite mass of Dartmoor, rising to 621m at High Willhays in the north west corner, can be a touch off-putting for those walkers who don't have the navigational ability or confidence to set off into the wilds across pathless ground. But around the edge of the open moor (particularly on the western and eastern sides) lies countryside that is undeniably some of the prettiest in Devon – if not the whole country – waiting to be explored via easy-to-follow paths and tracks. This is an exceptionally pretty Dartmoor walk on the western fringe of the moor that utilises the intricate network of paths originating from a time when this part of Devon was known for its important mining industry. The return stretch along Hill Bridge (or Wheal Friendship) Leat is a delight at all times of year, but especially for its springtime bluebells.

Map: OS Explorer 128 Dartmoor 1:25 000
Start point: Centre of Horndon. Grid ref: SX521800. Postcode PL19 9NQ
Directions to start: Horndon can be reached off the A386 (Okehampton to Tavistock road), turning off at Mary Tavy
Parking: On-road in hamlet – please exercise courtesy
Public Transport: Very limited buses, details at www.travelinesw.com. The nearest railway station is Gunnislake (8.2 miles)
Refreshments: The Elephant's Nest Inn, Horndon, 01822 810237
Toilets: None en route
Nearby places to stay: The Elephant's Nest Inn, Horndon, 01822 810237; Higher Rowes Farm, Horndon, 01822 810816; Homeleigh, Mary Tavy, 01822 810161
Nearby places of interest: Lydford Gorge (National Trust), Lydford, 01822 820320

From the three-way-junction in the centre of Horndon walk towards the telephone box (in the direction of Mary Tavy). At the T-junction turn left (dead end right) to reach The Elephant's Nest Inn.

Opposite the car park entrance look for a small public footpath sign right which directs you over the high hedgebank via a tricky and vertical climb

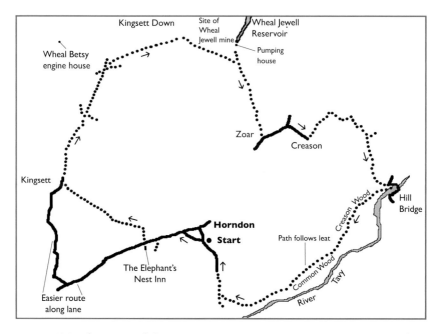

on small footholds: both hands and a good sense of balance required! (NB If this looks unappealing there's an easier option: keep straight on down the lane, taking the first right signed 'Kingsett', to rejoin the main route by Kingsett Farm: see map).

Keep along the right field edge, with views to Gibbet Hill (worth climbing on another occasion for its stunning 360-degree views) and Brentor's 13thC church of St. Michael de Rupe. Sited not on a granite tor but on a peak of solidified lava, this atmospheric little church is said to have been built by a mariner who, during a horrific storm at sea, swore to God that if He saved him he would build a church in His honour on a prominent spot. The Devil, however, had other ideas and hurled boulders on the unfortunate church builders from Cox Tor, a mile or two to the southeast! Cross the next difficult hedgebank; in the next field bear diagonally left, passing a small standing stone en route.

Just to the right of the far corner cross a wooden stile and another high hedgebank. Keep ahead and over another hedgebank via wooden ladders. Cross a stream (muddy) and keep ahead to tackle another hedgebank/ladder. Keep along the right edge of the next field; pass a gate (right), bearing left with the stream and hedgebank (right) to find a footbridge and stile into a large field.

Bear diagonally left, skirting boggy ground and aiming for a gate at the left end of a large barn in the centre of buildings at Kingsett Farm (thought by the late Dartmoor authority Eric Hemery possibly to have been a king's hunting seat in medieval times). Keep ahead through the farmyard, following the track right and left to reach the lane, near the ruins of 14th/15thC Lower Kingsett. Although thought to be a traditional longhouse dating from medieval times, an 1840s tithe map shows Lower Kingsett without the adjoining shippon: some believe that the latter was added to the farmhouse after a particularly bad winter and subsequent loss of stock. Whatever its history, the old farmhouse is today a sad and derelict place.

Turn right up the track, climbing gently to reach a gate onto Kingsett Down. Keep ahead, soon gaining views left to Wheal Betsy engine house (reopened in 1806, in operation until 1877) and Gibbet Hill. On reaching uneven ground (evidence of tin-mining activity associated with Wheal

Wheal Betsy engine house   *Kingsett Texels*

Zoar plus Cudlipptown Down landscape

Jewell) bear right to walk parallel to the wall along the edge of the down, picking up a track.

Follow the wall as it bears right, with views north towards Great Links, Sharp and Hare Tors. Closer to hand can be seen Wheal Jewell Reservoir (1936–7) and the remains of Wheal Jewell (reopened 1865, closed 1911), from where a leat descends to Wheal Betsy. At a wall corner keep ahead to pass below the pumping house to join a track leading from the reservoir. Turn right and drop to the lane opposite cottages at Zoar, almost ½ mile away.

View from the Creason turn

The industrial history of Mary Tavy

Three mines – Wheal Friendship, Wheal Betsy and Wheal Jewell (the latter two are passed on the route of this walk) – were in operation in this area during the 19thC when new water-powered technology enabled the more productive exploitation of a variety of minerals, in particular copper. Wheal Friendship was the largest of Dartmoor's copper mines. A look at the OS map reveals an intricate network of paths, dating no doubt from a time when locals walked through the fields to their place of work. Take a closer look and you'll be able to spot the thin blue lines denoting the leats which brought water from Dartmoor's rivers to power the revitalised mines. Wheal Betsy, whose iconic engine house is so visible to travellers on the A386 along the western side of the Moor, produced lead, copper, arsenic and silver. Wheal Jewell dates from the 18thC but was abandoned in 1797, reopened in 1865, and worked spasmodically in the early 20thC, largely for tin.

Walking beside the leat near Hill Bridge

Turn left, with views ahead towards Hare Tor, Ger Tor and the Tavy Cleave tors. At the junction turn right, signed 'Lower Creason'. At Creason Cottage turn left and follow the bridlepath rockily downhill between high hedgebanks past early 18thC Lowertown. Eventually go through a gate and field to pass Hill Bridge Old Schoolhouse (built 1835), later a chapel of ease (now a private house) to meet the lane. Keep ahead downhill towards the beautiful River Tavy.

Just before Hill Bridge turn right through a gate to reach the weir and take-off point of Hill Bridge Leat, which once carried water to the Wheal Friendship mining complex at Mary Tavy. Our peaceful path follows the deep fast-flowing leat downstream, initially parallel to the rushing waters of the Tavy. Continue on through Creason Wood (largely oak and beech), where the leat runs high up the valley side, with views through trees left to Cudlipptown Down. Continue through Common Wood, which is (from 2012) being managed for fritillary butterflies by the Dartmoor Preservation Association. Eventually cross a stile into a meadow, still following the leat.

Cross a wooden stile onto Horndon Lane (track); the leat continues ahead through private land to feed Bennett's reservoir. Turn right uphill to pass cottages and Furzemans Farm to find your car.

*Freelance editor and author **Sue Viccars** has lived on the edge of Dartmoor for more than thirty years, and has been editor of Dartmoor Magazine since 2008. Author of a large number of walking and holiday guides concentrating on the South West, she is also a regular contributor of walks to Exmoor the country magazine and Dartmoor Magazine. www.owpg.org.uk/member-profiles*

Walk 2
Ditsworthy Warren & 'War Horse' Country
by **Simon Dell**

Distance: 6 miles / 10km

This easy-going walk involves tracks and paths as well as some open moorland walking beside the River Plym. We will be visiting sites used in the filming of 'War Horse', the Stephen Spielberg movie based on Michael Morpurgo's much-loved novel. The walk does not venture into the military live training areas but you can reasonably expect to see soldiers training in groups in this area. They will not be using live ammunition.

Map: OS Outdoor Leisure 28 Dartmoor 1:25 000

Start point: Parking area at grid ref: SX578673

Directions to start: The parking area is at the end of the 'no-through' lane leading from Sheepstor Village

Parking: Small parking area at start point

Public Transport: The nearest railway station is Bere Ferrers (5.9 miles)

Refreshments: The Royal Oak, Meavy, 01822 852944

Toilets: None en route

Nearby places to stay: Callisham Farm, Meavy, 01822 853901; Pixeycombe, Meavy, 01822 853473; The Rosemont, Yelverton, 01822 852175

Nearby places of interest: Buckland Abbey (National Trust), Yelverton, 01822 853607

Note: Be aware: this route crosses open moorland, so a map and compass are necessary – and clear conditions. If you have a GPS it will be helpful

From the parking area walk south west towards Gutter Tor over the open grass area until you reach Sandy Path. Turn left along the path, more properly referred to as a rough Land Rover track with Gutter Tor on your right side.

As you look to the right there is a large fenced enclosure which ends at a point on Sandy Path where an ancient reeve or boundary crosses the path and heads uphill to the right towards the summit of Gutter Tor.

Just for a moment turn around and look back in the direction of the parked cars. On the other side of the road there are two fields separated

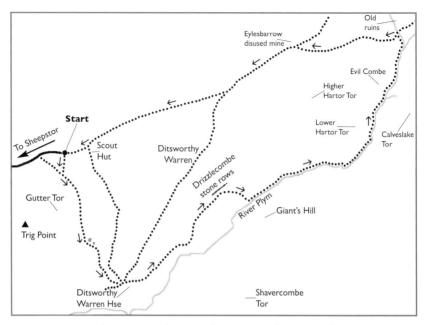

by a stone bank hedge. It is here at the start of the film where Albert was thrown from his horse Joey when Joey refused to jump the hedge.

As you follow the track there is plenty of evidence below you on the left of the work of the tinners; the streaming works and parallel mounds of spoil remaining from their quest for tin in the valley. The whole of this

Vermin trap

area was also used for the breeding of rabbits, hence the name given to the area of Ditsworthy Warren. To try to keep down the vermin (mainly stoats etc.) the warreners built traps of granite and wood. The remains of these traps are still to be seen around the valley on your left although many are in a ruinous condition. We are heading along the track to see one of these traps, which is situated on the slopes of Gutter Tor.

As you follow the track it goes around a sharp left hand bend. At this point turn right and go uphill, back towards the summit of Gutter Tor. The path here is a gentle grassy slope leading to the top of the tor. As you go up the path between the bracken, your route enters an area of clitter, or boulders, and the path gets steeper. At this point, as you come across

Ditsworthy Warren House

a wall ruin which crosses the pathway, look to your left beside the path and you will see a large boulder put up onto its side to form a funnelling wall which leads into the vermin trap about 8 paces from the path. The trap is capped with a granite slab and is only a few feet from the track.

Now return back down the grassy path to Sandy Path and to the bend, as the track goes down into the tinners' gully in the direction of Ditsworthy Warren House.

The track leads you through what would have been a gate and into the enclosure of Ditsworthy Warren. Ahead and to your left you will see the old Warren House start to appear. This is the building which was used in

Local industry
The whole of this area was worked by tin miners since the Bronze Age. The large gullies and mounds are all evidence of this industry. The area was also used until the end of the 19thC for the farming of rabbits and was known as a 'warren'. Many of these warrens can be found on Dartmoor. The dominating
hill overlooking much of this walk was mined until the mid 19thC, with deep mine shafts and mining ruins being easy to find.

the film where the Narracott family lived. Through the fields to left and right you will see the mounds of man-made rabbit warrens which housed the rabbits, known as 'pillow mounds' locally. The track leads you to the house, now a training centre bunkhouse for expeditions.

As you approach the Warren House you will see that it has a slate roof. In the film plastic thatch was added as well as shutters to the windows and flower boxes. The house is actually in private ownership belonging to the Maristowe Estate so entry to the enclosure is not allowed.

Below the house is a fenced field where Albert and Joey ploughed the turnip patch in the pouring rain. Look at the gnarled and twisted trees on the high Devon hedge bank below the house and you will recognise the tree which Albert climbed and sat in while Joey stretched his neck trying to reach him.

The gateway to the enclosure is featured prominently in the film and nothing had to be changed or repaired to make it authentic. Keep on the track and walk past the Warren House on your right, continuing along the path beside the enclosure to the rear of the house. If you take a look into the enclosure you will see several dog kennels built into the field walls.

Keep following the track with the Plym Valley way over to your right. Ahead is a hill sloping upwards away from you with the significant

Drizzlecombe Stone Rows. One of the largest standing stones on Dartmoor marks the end of one of these rows.

Once you have explored the stone row take a look at the nearby cairn then walk downhill towards the River Plym. We are now going to turn eastwards to walk up the Plym Valley where you will see what affect the tinners had in this area. Ahead of you and to the south of the river there are some large settlement circles. Our path runs beside the river now for about 2km (1¼ miles).

Take the higher of the paths to avoid the wet as you follow the river upstream, until you get to a point where the ground becomes quite boggy at a place known as Evil Combe. It is well worth avoiding walking straight across the 100 meters or so of the combe because it is very wet underfoot. Instead take a short detour and walk around it to the left keeping on the firm ground until you get to the other side and back on the banks of the Plym.

Continue upstream until you reach another smaller combe on your left (grid ref SX607681). Turn left into this small valley and head for some old

Dog kennel

Drizzlecombe standing stone

ruins, which are situated on a track at the head of the combe. This is where we turn left and westwards along the clearly defined path on the return journey back to the cars via the Eylesbarrow mine ruins.

The route follows the main track southwest back to the scout hut passing another mining ruin on your left. The track is now back to the standard of a rough Land Rover track and leads you downhill to the enclosure by the trees where you left your car some hours ago.

Mine ruins

Simon Dell MBE *is a retired policeman and is now working as a guide on Dartmoor and also Lundy Island. He runs Moorland Guides www.moorlandguides.co.uk – a small guiding company employing over 40 guides. Simon is the author of numerous books about Dartmoor, Industrial Archaeology, Lundy and social history. He writes for the BBC Countryfile Magazine as well as other journals.*

Walk 3
Otterton & the River Otter
by **Belinda Whitworth**

Distance: 4¾ or 5½ miles / 7.6 or 8.9 km

This is an exceptionally pretty walk which starts along the River Otter and continues through shady paths and across farmland, with wide views of both the sea and the glorious East Devon countryside. Well-marked paths and easy terrain, but muddy in places. A working watermill with above-average food to tempt you en route.

Map: OS Explorer 115 Exmouth & Sidmouth 1:25 000
Start point: White Bridge, near Budleigh Salterton. Grid ref: SY074830.
Postcode (nearest): EX9 7AY
Directions to start: Coming into Budleigh Salterton on B3178 from East Budleigh, pass 30mph sign and town sign. Immediately turn left, and immediately left again along South Farm Road. Follow road for ½ mile until you reach bridge
Parking: In small areas off the road before or past White Bridge
Public Transport: Otterton and Budleigh Salterton are served by buses run by Stagecoach South West and Axe Valley Mini-Travel, timetables available at www.travelinesw.com. The nearest railway station is at Exmouth (5.8 miles)
Refreshments: Kings Arms, Fore Street, Otterton, 01395 568416; Otterton Mill, Otterton, 01395 567041
Toilets: At Otterton Mill for customers
Nearby places to stay: Heath Close, 3 Lansdowne Road, Budleigh Salterton, 01395 444337; The Kings Arms, Otterton, 01395 568416; Stoneborough House, 21a East Budleigh Road, Budleigh Salterton, 01395 445923
Nearby places of interest: Fairlynch Museum, 27 Fore Street, Budleigh Salterton, 01395 442666; Otterton Mill, Otterton, 01395 567041

At White Bridge take the footpath to the right (north), upriver and away from the sea. (The footpath towards the sea goes through an Estuary Nature Reserve. Another day.) You will now find yourself on a wide gravelled path, rebuilt in spring 2013 after floods washed it away. This part of the walk is deservedly popular. (Later paths are quieter, but no less lovely.)

As you walk, watch for the flash of turquoise that is a kingfisher, or the swallows skimming the water in spring and summer. Wildflowers

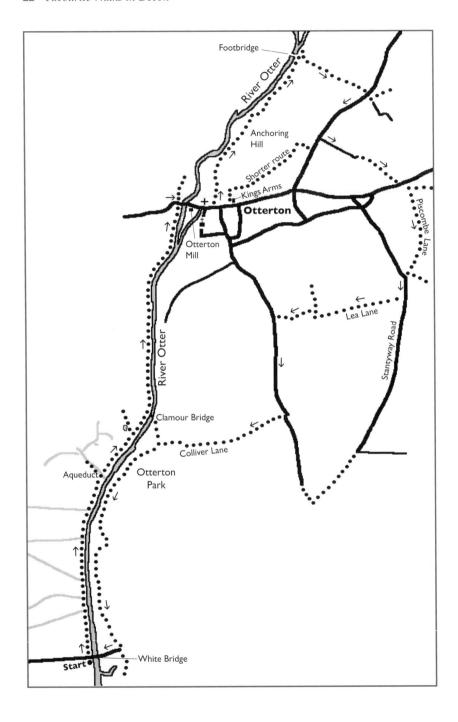

abound – particularly in the water meadows to your left. In spring, note the giant yellow blobs of kingcups (marsh marigold) and the lilac carpets of lady's smock (cuckoo flower).

In about ten minutes you will come to a kissing gate. Go through it and across the aqueduct, built in the early 19thC to drain the water meadows. Walk across the field, keeping close to the river, until you come to a footbridge. This is Clamour Bridge. Ignore it and carry on through the gate and along the riverside path. In another ten minutes or so you will come to a road. Turn right and cross the roadbridge. (This is a bit hairy as the road is narrow and busy and there's no pavement.) You are now in the village of Otterton. Turn immediately right into Otterton Mill for refreshment.

White Bridge on the River Otter, the beginning of your walk

Once refreshed, and if you can still move, leave the Mill and turn right. You now have two choices – the longer more beautiful route or the shorter one.

Shorter route: *Go past the green and take the footpath through the car park of the Kings Arms pub. Follow this up a short flight of steps and the pub garden and then to the right along the back of houses. Cross a stile and walk along the bottom of the field, turning diagonally left at the electricity pole. Through the gate turn right, cross the field and climb a stile. Descend the path (past Anchoring Cottage on your left) and at the road turn left. After about 60 paces turn right on to a track marked as a public footpath. Continue from (*) below.*

The River Otter in springtime – ideal habitat for otters

Longer route: Take the first footpath on your left across the green. Go over the stream, past the house, up the grassy path and through the gate ahead. The river is now on your left at the bottom of a sheer drop. When seasonal foliage allows note the weir with a special stepped channel for salmon travelling up-river to spawn. On your right is Anchoring Hill, so called because in medieval times the river was navigable to here and boats used the hill as a marker.

Go through another gate and follow the lower edge of the field (with a small wooded hill to your right) until you come to a footbridge over the river. Don't cross it but instead go through the metal gates ahead and down on to a new footpath where you turn right. Climb the path, pausing to look at the views of rolling farmland. The path then widens into a track and goes downhill to join a lane. Turn right on to the lane and follow it back towards the village (caution with traffic). Pass North Star Engineering on your right and then take the next track to the left. It is marked as a public footpath.

(*) Shorter and longer routes now merge. Climb the track and when you get to the field turn right. Follow the field edge up the hill, enjoying the views to your left. Go through the gate at the top right corner of the field onto a small path which leads to a road, where you turn left. After 50 or so paces, and just before the sign marking the end of the speed limit, turn right into a lane (Piscombe Lane on Explorer map). The lane soon

Otters and water voles

Otters do live and breed on the River Otter but if you see one of these beautiful and intelligent animals you're very lucky as they are shy and largely nocturnal. By the 1970s they had disappeared from many British rivers but with a ban on their hunting (in 1978) as well as improvements to water quality and habitat they have made a comeback. Devon now has more otters than any other lowland part of the UK and an internationally important population. They are still, however, a protected species. Until recently water voles were extinct in Devon, having all been eaten by mink escaped from fur farms. However these endearing little mammals (which look like miniature beavers) have recently been successfully reintroduced to a protected area on the River Tale – which joins the Otter further north. Efforts are underway to remove mink from the River Otter in the hope that the voles will make their own way into it.

becomes a track. Keep on it until you come to a crossroads. Carry on in the same direction taking the road away from Otterton (Stantyway Road on Explorer map). You will now have views of the sea.

Soon you will come to a right turning marked 'Unmetalled road' (Lea Lane on Explorer map). Take this and follow it round to the right then, where there is also an option to go straight ahead, follow it round to the left until you reach a lane. Here turn left.

One of the lovely paths that take you around the outside of the village of Otterton

Walk down the lane and at the bottom where it bends right take a right-hand path marked 'Bridleway to Clamour Bridge' (Colliver Lane on map). Follow the path through two gates and round a field edge, noting the mature trees on your left – part of Otterton Park.

Cut through the bank on to a small lane (or, if you want to be law-abiding, carry on round the field until the path reaches the lane). This delightful lane – lined with wildflowers in spring and summer – is closed to cars. Go left and it will take you all the way back to White Bridge.

The delightful lane that takes you back to your start point

Belinda Whitworth *has lived in rural Devon since 1978 and walks in it every day (if she can). Having worked as a book editor and non-fiction writer for twenty years, specialising in complementary health and the environment, she is now exploring fiction writing. See Belinda's blog 'Mad Englishwoman and Dog' (www.belinda-whitworth.blogspot.co.uk) for more.*

Walk 4
Thorverton & Raddon Hills
by **Simone Stanbrook-Byrne**

Distance: 6 miles / 10km

This fabulous walk rewards you with some of the most astonishing views you'll find in Mid Devon. The outward journey is uphill at times, but it's very much worth the effort and it's downhill nearly all the way back. Listen out for the mew of buzzards, the cronk of ravens and, in summer, the song of skylarks.

Map: OS Explorer 114, Exeter & the Exe Valley 1:25 000	
Start point: Thorverton Village Car Park. Grid ref SS923021. Postcode EX5 5NG.	
Directions to start: Thorverton is clearly signposted off the A396 Exeter-Tiverton road. Turn left at The Ruffwell Inn	
Parking: The free car park is signed from the village centre	
Public Transport: This area is served by buses from Exeter and Tiverton, details available at www.travelinesw.com. The nearest railway stations are Newton St. Cyres (3.4 miles) and Exeter St. David's (5½ miles)	
Refreshments: The Ruffwell, Thorverton, 01392 860377, which is on the A396 rather than in the village centre; The Thorverton Arms, 01392 860205	
Toilets: None	
Nearby places to stay: The Thorverton Arms, 01392 860205	
Nearby places of interest: Killerton (NT), Broadclyst, 01392 881345	

Leave the car park and turn right on the lane heading uphill out of the village. The lane levels out and ahead of you up on the hillside you see a lone pine, which you will meet later. Continue on the lane passing, on your right, the red brick house of Lynch Farm, with its striking monkey puzzle tree. Three quarters of a mile from the car park you reach Chapel Corner (Chapel Cross on OS map). Continue ahead here towards Shobrooke and Crediton and after another 150m you will see a kissing gate on your right, just past farm buildings and opposite a modern house. Go through here and bear slightly left through the field to follow the boundary on your left. This leads to another kissing gate, go through and continue ahead with the fence to your left and a copse to your right. The path bears slightly right to pass through the end of the copse and brings you to a gate.

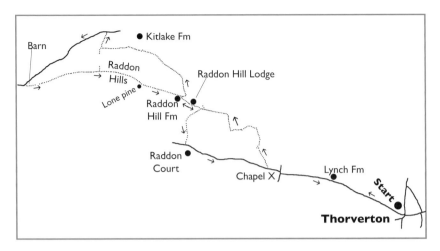

Beyond here turn immediately left through another gate, hop over a small stream and then turn right to walk up this field with the boundary on your right. Turn left with the boundary at the top of the field and keep beside it until the footpath exits right. Cross into the next field and turn left, keeping the hedge on your left and follow it round as it skirts the field, until, in the top left corner, you find footpath access into the next field. Pass through here and bear diagonally up in the direction of the yellow arrow. You will see a waymarker post part way across the field to help guide you. In the top corner, diagonally opposite the point at which you entered, you will find a stile to lead you out of the field. Glance behind you here towards the south east. There are vast views and the Sidmouth Gap is clearly noticeable in the distance.

After the stile you meet a track. Walk straight ahead down to a gate about 30m away. Beyond here turn right along the surfaced drive, to pass the wonderfully-located Raddon Hill Lodge with its stunning views. The public footpath goes straight past their garden, respect their privacy please. Keep ahead on the track past the house and very soon you reach the buildings of Raddon Hill Farm at which point the track turns sharp right. Go with it, ignoring a footpath up steps to your left and continuing a short distance along the track to a gate on the left with yellow arrows.

Pass through here and head straight up the next field with the boundary on your right – away to your left from here you can see the top section of the lone pine. The field levels out towards the top and ahead of you slightly to the left you will see another yellow-arrowed gate leading left onto a narrow path. Before passing through the gate to join this, enjoy views to the north-east and the early Iron Age hill fort of Cadbury Castle.

Once you've looked your fill, join the path which is narrow and wends its way between hedges. From time to time you will find gates to negotiate but the yellow arrows direct you straight on, don't be tempted to veer up left into the fields. Eventually you see the buildings of Kitlake Farm down to your right. When you are almost level with Kitlake you

Towards the Iron Age hill fort of Cadbury Castle

meet another gate and the yellow arrow now directs you left to a small gate through which you leave this narrow path – don't be tempted to leave it any earlier than this.

Once you're through this gate go immediately right to follow the field boundary on your right. After about 50m you reach another yellow-arrowed gate. Pass through and continue ahead with the boundary on your right until you reach the end of the next field. Here turn right and walk down the next field to the stile which you will see in the bottom left corner. There are more good views across to Cadbury Castle from here – look out for the dragon (see feature, page 32).

After the stile turn left along the lane heading away from Kitlake Farm. Follow this for just over half a mile. You start to climb slightly and as the route flattens out again you will see the back of a corrugated barn on your left. As the lane bears right look out for a footpath sign pointing sharp left off the lane, back on yourself. Take this path, now passing the open front of the barn on your left, and continue ahead through the field with the hedge on your right. This is an elevated and airy stretch of walking with panoramic 360° views and windswept trees. It can be wonderfully wild up here in some weathers. Behind you to the right you can see Dartmoor.

Lone pine on Raddon Hills

Eventually you pass through another gate into the next field. Continue in the same direction to the gates ahead of you and through them into a third field. In this field continue ahead but now with the boundary on your left. Head towards the massive pine tree – you can't miss it. A long time ago there were more of these trees standing here: this survivor now stands as lone sentinel over Raddon Hills. A majestic sight. Hug it, if you are so inclined, the tree deserves it.

From here head to the stile beyond the tree, cross it and bear diagonally right down the next field to a stile in the bottom boundary. This leads to the steps which you passed earlier. Go down them, turning right at the

Walking across Raddon Hills

bottom to retrace your steps along the track past Raddon Hill Farm and Raddon Hill Lodge.

Beyond Raddon Hill Lodge you have an option. When you reach the bend in their drive you can either go left to pick up the footpath which you came along earlier, retracing your steps along your outward route, or continue all the way down the increasingly stony drive beyond Raddon Lodge until you meet the lane. At the lane turn left, passing Raddon Court on your right which you may have noticed during the course of the walk from the elevated paths you have been on above it. Follow this lane all the way back to Thorverton and your car.

The Killerton Dragon

Legend has it that the Iron Age hill forts at Cadbury and Dolbury (part of the Killerton estate) each conceal hidden treasure. The Killerton Dragon guards both, flying nightly between the two, a distance of some six miles as dragons fly. In addition to his duties on the hill forts, the dragon is reputedly also the protector of the family at Fursdon House, not far from Cadbury. Occasionally one hears dissent about whether the dragon actually belongs to Killerton or Cadbury. The dragon knows for a fact that he isn't owned by anybody.

Simone Stanbrook-Byrne wrote her first guide for Mid Devon in 2000. In 2010 she teamed up with James Clancy to form Culm Valley Publishing which specialises in outdoor leisure guides for the West Country. Together they produce an expanding series of books for the region: www.culmvalleypublishing.co.uk

Barnstaple
by James Clancy

Distance: 2 miles / 3.2km

Many of Devon's towns lend themselves to on-foot exploration and Barnstaple has some beautiful buildings and a wealth of history. During the 11thC it had its own mint and in the Middle Ages it was a staple port for wool export, a trade which brought great wealth to the town. Many of the buildings, including the market, the clock tower and Bridge Chambers, were designed by the 19thC borough surveyor, Richard Gould. This is an easy, level route, the only hill being encountered if you decide on the brief excursion to the top of the castle mound at the end of the walk.

Start point: Cattle Market Car Park, Holland Street, EX31 1DP

Directions to start: Barnstaple is situated in North Devon, 34 miles north west of Exeter. Major roads that converge on the town are the A39, A361 and A377

Parking: Cattle Market Car Park, Holland Street

Public transport: There are numerous bus connections to and from Barnstaple with services run by FirstGroup and Stagecoach Devon amongst others. Timetables available online at www.travelinesw.com. Barnstaple railway station is located at Station Road

Refreshments: The Cream Tea Café, Church Lane, 01271 325727; Driftwood Café, Gammon Walk, 01271 329488

Toilets: Cattle Market Car Park and pannier market

Nearby places to stay: The Imperial Hotel, Taw Vale Parade, 01271 345861; The Old Post Office, 22 Pilton Street, 01271 859439; Sunnymead B&B, 2 Sunnymead, 01271 325254

Nearby places of interest: Broomhill Sculpture Gardens, Muddiford, 01271 850262; Museum of Barnstaple and North Devon, The Square, 01271 346747

Market days: General market: Tuesday, Friday and Saturday. Craft and General Market: Monday (April to Christmas) and Thursday; Antiques & Collectables: Wednesday

Start by walking across the car park, away from the public loos and towards a red brick building with rounded walls. At the road by this building cross over and turn left. Pass the old station building on the right and go right beyond it towards the River Taw. Lean on the railings and

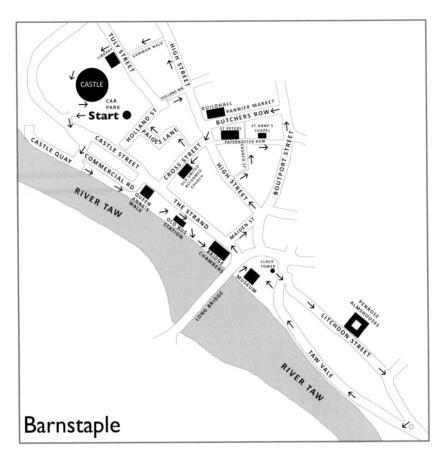

Barnstaple

look right towards the clean lines of the modern bridge, then turn left and walk along the path towards the lovely old bridge which dates back to the 15thC. Keep the river to your right.

> **Bridge:** *The old bridge, also known as 'Long Bridge', is first mentioned in records dating back to around the 13thC. It has been modified and widened over the centuries*

You reach the colonnaded building of Queen Anne's Walk (the colonnades are on the side away from you as you approach). Turn left to walk past its front, then go right along the road (Castle Street) as far as The Old Bus Station, once a railway station. Admire its façade then turn right to re-join the riverside path, continuing with the river on your right and passing behind the grand buildings of the Bridge Chambers. Walk under the old bridge and go left up steps immediately after it. These lead to the Museum of Barnstaple and North Devon, which also houses an information centre. At the end of the building turn right towards the clock tower, built as a memorial to Prince Albert in 1862 and restored in 2009.

Queen Anne's Walk was once a merchant's 'exchange' adjacent to the quay. Dating back to the early 18thC, it is Grade 1 listed and is on the site of an earlier exchange. The building behind the colonnades was built in 1850 and has had a variety of uses including that of bath house and Masonic lodge

Brannam's Pottery (top left); Long Bridge (top right); Queen Anne's Walk (above)

Clock Tower   St. Peter's Church

Great Quay was built in 1550 and was situated in front of Queen Anne's Walk. In the 16th–17thC Barnstaple was a great centre of commerce, importing wine, tobacco and spices as well as boodle from privateering! The main export products were wool and pottery. Great Quay was one of the facilities built to accommodate the ships which plied their trade and from here, in 1588, five ships sailed to fight the Spanish Armada. By 1850 the river was so silted up that the quay was no longer in use and so was filled in. A railway station was constructed on the site

---

Continue in the same direction beyond the clock tower, crossing the road and walking ahead down Litchdon Street, the Imperial Hotel is on your right. A short way down you will find the beautiful buildings where Brannam's pottery had its being until 1990. It now houses a hairdresser's. Look up to admire the stained glass on the first floor.

Just beyond here you will find the venerable Penrose Almshouses, notice their little bell tower at the far end. Continue to the end of Litchdon Street, ignoring a road coming in from the left, and you will reach a junction with New Road and Taw Vale. Turn sharp right here and cross over towards the pinnacle which marks the end of Rock Park – one William Frederick Rock presented the park to the people in 1879. Walk away from the pinnacle, back along the river, which is to your left – you are now approaching the old bridge from its other side.

Penrose Almshouses *were founded in the 17thC by John Penrose, a successful merchant and sometime mayor who bequeathed money for their construction. The eagle-eyed might spot bullet holes dating back to the Civil War. The almshouses are Grade l listed*

There are some lovely, balconied houses to your right as you progress along here, culminating in the front façade of the Imperial Hotel. Return to the clock tower and from it walk ahead, passing the museum and information centre on your left. Cross the road and continue along the front of the Bridge Chambers. This is now The Strand. Opposite the Bridge Chambers' entrance turn right off The Strand along Maiden Street. At the end of Maiden Street glance across to The Bank restaurant, once a 17thC merchant's house. It has a fabulous ceiling if you peek inside. From Maiden Street turn left and left again up High Street and within 100m turn right along the very narrow Church Lane.

As this lane bends left notice the old school on the right followed by the Horwood Almshouses and the Paige Almshouses. Beyond here you meet

Penrose Almshouses

Church Lane

a crossing of paths. Go left, this is Paternoster Row, and visit the Grade ll* listed parish church of St. Peter, with its golden weather vane and twisted spire, caused by the lead warping in the heat of the sun.

Come out of the church and turn left back along Paternoster Row, walking past Church Lane and continuing ahead on the path between two ancient buildings: St. Anne's Chapel on the left and the younger Parish Hall on the right.

Church Lane and Paternoster Row *are teeming with history. The old Horwood School was founded in 1659 by Alice Horwood for "20 poor maids". The girls were taught to sew and read but not to write. Priorities were very different then. It functioned as a school until 1814 and the building was restored in 1917. Beyond this are the Horwood Almshouses, founded by the wealthy merchant Thomas Horwood, also in the mid 17thC, and completed by his wife. These were to house 16 people whereas the Paige's Almshouses next door, founded by Elizabeth Paige in 1656, were for just 8 residents. These were built on the site of even older almshouses. All these buildings are Grade ll* listed. Beyond the almshouses the paths are surrounded by raised ground. This is due to the area having been a burial site for many centuries, with surplus soil being scattered over the ground after burials, gradually raising the level. There has been a church on the site of St. Peter's in Paternoster Row since Saxon* *times, the original building would have been wooden. The present church dates back to the 14thC with many successive alterations over the centuries. The Grade 1 listed St. Anne's Chapel is thought to have originated in the 14thC although the crypt is much older and may once have functioned as a charnel house. The chapel building also served as a grammar school from the mid 16thC to the early 20thC. John Gay, composer of The Beggar's Opera, was educated here. The building on the opposite side of Paternoster Row from St. Anne's is now a very active Parish Hall*

At the end of the path turn left along Boutport Street, one of the main shopping areas, and within 100m go left along the quaint Butchers' Row with its Mecca of tiny, independent shops on the left hand side and the bustling pannier market on the right. Both are worth a browse. At the end of Butchers' Row notice the 1827 Guildhall on the right hand corner then turn left along High Street followed by the next right down Cross Street.

Butchers' Row is a series of small, delightful shops built of Bath stone in 1855. Few of them remain as butchers and nowadays they are a good source of artisan foods. Previously the butchers' market was held where The Guildhall and part of the pannier market now stand

Pannier Market: A market place has existed in this town since Saxon times. The pannier market building was constructed in 1855 to replace the previous outdoor market which was held along the High Street and fell short of hygiene requirements even for those days. Originally it was primarily for the sale of vegetables. The name derives from the panniers or baskets in which goods were once brought to market, long before a building such as this existed

A short way down Cross Street you will find the Grade ll listed building of the old United Reformed Church on the left. This ceased to be a church over 20 years ago and now houses an antiques centre. Their antiques are worth browsing, as is the interior of this delightful building. Leave the building, turning right to retrace your steps along Cross Street for about 30m, crossing the road and taking the first left along a narrow way until it emerges near the car park. This is Paiges Lane.

Turn right at the car park, this is Holland Street, and keep ahead as it enters the narrow Holland Walk. At the end turn left along High Street, passing the modern Green Lanes Shopping Centre on the right. Soon you reach the pedestrianised Gammon Walk on the left. Take this, first noticing the ornate façade of the shop on the corner. At the end of Gammon Walk turn right and walk past the library and record office, then turn left around the end of the building to approach the open space of Barnstaple's old motte and bailey castle. Explore the surroundings here as several information boards give interesting details about the history of the area.

A clear path winds up to the top of the castle which I recommend you ascend. You're standing on centuries of history up here although a blind eye has to be turned to any 21stC litter. Descend by the same path to walk anticlockwise around the mound and back to the car park.

Barnstaple Castle was a 'motte and bailey' design, which comprised a wooden keep on a mound or 'motte' surrounded by an enclosure or 'bailey'. The first wooden castle was constructed here in the 11thC, with a stone building the following century, but by the 14thC the building was falling into ruin. The 'motte' is the most visible remnant today. Much of the stone was removed for building purposes elsewhere in the area. Prior to the Norman Conquest the area was an Anglo Saxon burial site

James Clancy has co-authored 9 walking books with Simone Stanbrook-Byrne. Together they founded Culm Valley Publishing, which specialises in walking guides for the South West (www.culmvalleypublishing.co.uk). James has always enjoyed exploring this region and capturing the variety of scenery on offer with his trusty Canon EOS camera.

Walk 6
Exploring the Hartland Peninsula
by **Sue Viccars**

Distance: 4 or 5 miles / 6.5 or 8km

One of the most important things to think about when working out a circular route along the South West Coast Path is how to make the inland stretch as appealing as the coastal section, and this example on the Hartland Peninsula manages pretty well! This part of the North Devon coast is blessed with a number of high-hedged, sheltered green lanes running parallel to the coast, in tranquil contrast with the tortured and wind-blasted cliffs, enabling the creation of some wonderful circular routes. This is a surprisingly moderate walk that experiences the very best of Devon's northwest tip: the spectacular cliffs and hanging valleys around historic Hartland Quay, with a gentle return along the sheltered valley of the Abbey River.

Map: OS Explorer 126 Clovelly & Hartland
Start point: St. Nectan's Church, Stoke, nr Hartland. Grid ref: SS235247. Postcode: EX39 6DU. (NB. The route can also be started from Hartland Quay: small parking fee April–October, 10am–3pm)
Directions to start: Situated in the north west tip of Devon, Stoke is slightly west of the village of Hartland and can be accessed via the A39 and the B3248
Parking: On road near church – please exercise courtesy
Public Transport: Buses serve the nearby village of Hartland, details available at www.travelinesw.com. The nearest railway station is Barnstaple (19 miles)
Refreshments: Docton Mill, 01237 441369; Hartland Quay Hotel, 01237 441218
Toilets: Stoke and Hartland Quay
Nearby places to stay: Golden Park, Hartland, 01237 441254; Hartland Quay Hotel, 01237 441218
Nearby places of interest: Docton Mill Gardens, Lymebridge, 01237 441369; Hartland Abbey, Hartland, 01237 441234

This walk starts from the south door of St. Nectan's Church, dating from the 14thC and known as 'the Cathedral of North Devon' on account of its imposing location. (About 100m east of the church can be found St. Nectan's Well, said to be the site of the Celtic saint's hermitage.) Facing the church, turn right through the churchyard, leaving it via the lychgate (or broad stone stile and steps) to reach the lane (toilets left). Keep ahead

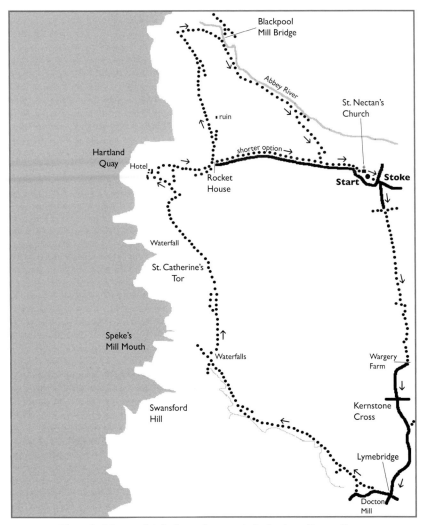

passing Church House (right), and turn right before Rose Cottage on an initially tarmac lane that rises gently. At the next junction keep ahead on a green lane between hedgebanks thick with wildflowers in late spring: bluebells, dog violets, red campion, buttercups, greater stitchwort... Eventually the track levels off, then descends steeply into a wooded combe and crosses a stream. Ascend to reach the entrance to Wargery Farm. Bear right along the farm drive to reach a crossroads of lanes at Kernstone Cross.

Keep ahead, following signs for Docton Mill and Elmscott, soon dropping downhill (enjoying the heady almond scents of warm gorse blossom in early summer sunshine) to a crossroads of lanes (and pretty cottages) at Lymebridge. *If it's not too early for a refreshment break, keep ahead for 20m to find beautiful Docton Mill and Gardens; entry to tearooms free. The Domesday Book of 1086 refers to a mill in this area; the last working miller bought Docton Mill in 1895, but it closed in 1910 in the face of cheaper imports from Canada.*

Turn right at the crossroads, signed Milford. The lane soon bears left: turn right as signed on a track, alongside a stream. Pass the entrance to Milford Mill, and follow the track (wet in patches) along the valley bottom through light woodland, eventually passing through a gate at a cattle grid into Speke's Mill Valley, now in open ground. Lofty Swansford Hill, which towers above the sea, comes into view ahead. The valley broadens, and the stream meanders across level ground. Stay on the track as it ascends slightly, joining the coast path then levelling en route to the coast at Speke's Mill Mouth: take some time to marvel at the waterfalls and sheer cliffs here. In early summer enjoy carpets of pink sea thrift, yellow kidney vetch and white ox-eye daisies. There is access to the rocky beach below via long flights of wooden steps.

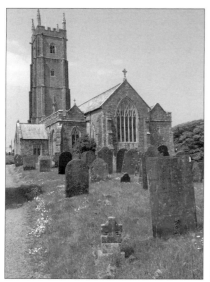

St. Nectan's Church
Waterfall at Speke's Mill

Hartland Quay

As well as being blessed with an incredible geology in the form of a succession of vertical coastal tiltings and contortions dating back some 300 million years, the Hartland Peninsula also has a long and fascinating history: it was known as the 'Promontory of Hercules' by the 2ndC Greek astronomer Ptolemy. The extraordinarily atmospheric Hartland Quay, too, is worthy of further examination. Dating from 1586, when communications by land in this remotest corner of Devon were virtually non-  existent and heavy goods had to be shipped in and landed on this inhospitable coast, it's easy today to transport yourself back to a time when the quay was buzzing with commercial activity. Coal, slate and lime were shipped in, and local produce such as barley and oats shipped out. Traffic was much reduced when the railway reached Bideford in 1855, but the quay was active until the late 19thC when the harbour wall finally succumbed to the ravages of the sea. Some of the buildings were converted to a hotel at the end of the 19thC.

Pick up the coast path as it runs north (sea to your left) up the cliff via rough steps, then a rough and rocky path. The coastal scenery ahead is mind-blowing! Pass through a gate onto the open cliff top and follow the dilapidated cliff-edge fence over close-cropped turf, studded with daisies. Note ahead right the tower of St. Nectan's Church, said to be the second tallest in Devon. The massive pyramidal coastal hill seen ahead, its seaward side collapsed into the sea, is St. Catherine's Tor: rising 84m above sea level, it is named after a chapel which once crowned its summit.

The coast path drops steeply then bears inland to pass through a small gate. Cross a level meadow, and a stream, aiming for a gate between the bottom right edge of St. Catherine's Tor and a substantial restored hedgebank. Wander over to the cliff edge to find another waterfall, then continue on the coast path: look back south to see a stunning succession of coastal headlands (including Henna Cliff at Morwenstow, the highest sheer cliff in England after Beachy Head) stretching towards Bude in north Cornwall.

Suddenly the buildings at Hartland Quay come into view below left, with far-ranging views across the ocean to mystical Lundy Island, lying 12 miles off Hartland Point. The coast path runs inland and through a kissing gate, then returns to the cliff edge above Well Beach and ascends a short flight of steps. Walk along the edge of a level parking area, then drop down rough steps to reach Hartland Quay. Look out for blue squill and bladder (sea) campion, kidney vetch and thrift.

Turn right to ascend the lane behind the hotel. Opposite the first parking area take the coast path (signed on the left) and climb steeply up a narrow path through gorse and blackthorn to meet the lane by the Rocket House (built soon after the SS Uppingham was stranded under Longapeak in 1890 to house essential lifesaving equipment). *To shorten the walk slightly keep ahead along the lane for a few paces, then turn left through a gate and immediately right: follow the right field edge back to St. Nectan's Church.*

Turn left before the Rocket House through a gate and walk along the level cliff top – known as The Warren, and once used for farming rabbits – soon passing the ruins of the 'Pleasure House', originally built as a two-storey lookout for spying on smugglers and incoming ships, and later used as a summerhouse by the residents of nearby Hartland Abbey, the latter built in 1779 on the site of an Augustinian foundation. Views open up ahead over Blegberry Beach and the impressive coastline north towards

Coast path to Blackpool Mill Cottage

Abbey River woodland

Hartland Point, and lovely Blackpool Mill Cottage (a former grist mill dating from at least the 16thC) nestled in the valley of the Abbey River below. Sweep down into the combe, turning inland through dense blackthorn and honeysuckle and through a gate to meet a path junction at Blackpool Mill Bridge.

The coast path turns left across the Abbey River, but we keep ahead through glorious light woodland thick with bluebells, wild garlic and pink purslane in May. Note the wonderfully windblown twisted beech trees, near which a fenced and stepped section rounds a landslip caused by heavy rains late in 2012. Leave the woodland and keep along the bottom edge of a field. Where the path ducks back under the trees bear right uphill along the field edge.

At the top corner turn left through a small gate just before reaching the lane, and along a narrow path. Cross a stone stile and pass the Coastguard Cottages to reach a track: turn right along the church wall, then left over a stone stile back into the churchyard and the start point.

Freelance editor and author **Sue Viccars** *has lived on the edge of Dartmoor for more than thirty years, and has been editor of Dartmoor Magazine since 2008. Author of a large number of walking and holiday guides concentrating on the South West, she is also a regular contributor of walks to Exmoor the country magazine and Dartmoor Magazine. www.owpg.org.uk/member-profiles*

Walk 7
Above & Beside the River Erme
by **Adam Hart-Davis** *(with original sketches)*

Distance: 3¾ or 5.6 miles / 6 or 9km

This walk entails climbing to a ridge to gain fine views of the south-western corner of Dartmoor, and (briefly) of the sea to the south; descending to the village of Ermington; climbing a long gentle road, and following the Erme-Plym trail down to a path beside the River Erme, with possible sightings of various river birds and fish. Possible birds throughout the walk include: blackbird, blue tit, buzzard, Canada goose, carrion crow, chaffinch, cormorant, dipper, dunnock, goldfinch, goosander, great tit, grey wagtail, gulls, house sparrow, jackdaw, kestrel, kingfisher, long-tailed tit, magpie, mallard, pied wagtail, raven, robin, rook, shelduck, skylark, sparrowhawk, swallow, swift, woodpigeon and wren.

Map: OS Explorer OL20 South Devon, Brixham to Newton Ferrers 1:25 000
Start point: South Devon Tennis Centre, Ivybridge. Grid ref: SX633555. Postcode: PL21 9ES
Directions to start: Ivybridge is in the south-west corner of Devon, to the east of Plymouth
Parking: Car park serving South Devon Tennis Centre / Ivybridge Town FC (by kind permission of South Hams District Council and the Tennis Centre)
Public Transport: Ivybridge is well served by buses from the following operators: Plymouth Citybus, First in Devon & Cornwall, Tally Ho!, Stagecoach South West. Timetables available at www.travelinesw.com. Ivybridge has a railway station
Refreshments: The Crooked Spire, Ermington, 01548 831288; various options in Ivybridge
Toilets: On Town Hill close to The Crooked Spire in Ermington
Nearby places to stay: Cadleigh Manor Hotel, Cadleigh, Ivybridge, 01752 895678; Plantation Hotel (expensive but excellent), Ermington, 01548 831100; Sportsman Inn, Ivybridge, 01752 892280
Nearby places of interest: Saltram House, Plymouth, 01752 333503; Buckland Abbey, Yelverton, 01822 853607 (both National Trust)

From the tennis centre car park take the path north-west beside the children's playground. When you get to the river, turn right (on the coast-to-coast Erme-Plym trail) under the road beside the river and emerge opposite the recycling centre. Turn right and right again, to walk along the pavement, on the right-hand side of the busy road and across the river.

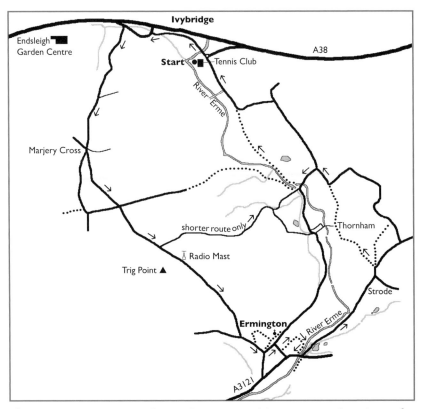

The River Erme is usually a pleasant tumbling stream, but from the scouring of the banks and the trees and boulders that have been washed downstream you can see how violent it can be in spate. Said to be the second fastest river in England, it rises 10km north, on Dartmoor, and flows about 9km south, to emerge between Wonwell Beach and Mothercombe.

Pass Antique Bathrooms and David May Motors on your right and an industrial estate on your left. This is the least pleasant section of the walk because of the relentless noise of traffic on the A38. At the T-junction (marked A38 in both directions) turn left for the Endsleigh Garden Centre. Go down the slip road and turn left for Westlake. Then do not turn right for Endsleigh; instead keep straight on up the hill. This is a tough ten minute climb, but the compensation is that the noise from the A38 rapidly fades; by the time you are over the top of the hill it is barely a whisper; you begin to hear the birds around you, and the view improves.

500m later you reach Marjery Cross, with a postbox and a rickety signpost. Go straight across, on the road for Westlake and Ermington, but after only 10m take the left fork on to an unmarked road. You are now in riding country, and you may see evidence of horses on either side.

The road climbs slowly upward towards a radio mast, and a magnificent view opens up on the left, with the barren mound of Western Beacon looming above the long straggle of Ivybridge, as it huddles below the southern slopes of Dartmoor. To the far left are china clay quarries – porcelain was first made in England by William Cookworthy, who built a factory in Plymouth in 1768. To the right is the village of Bittaford, below the long dark structure of Moorhaven, built as a Victorian lunatic asylum.

Birds chatter and mock from the hedges; pass the crossroads, and as you climb higher the view begins to open up on the right as well, until from the gateway 20m before the radio mast you can see the sea, 8km due south. A few metres further on a new view appears in front: Ermington Woods across the valley, above and beyond them a corner of Modbury, patchwork fields and high ridges.

For a 3km short cut, turn back the way you came, and 200m down the road turn right on to another unmarked road. Half way down the steep hill note the isolated "witch's house". A hermit lived here for 40 years, but it was recently sold and will probably be rebuilt. A gateway further down on the right provides a view of the village of Penquit across the valley.

Witch's House

*In the hamlet of Higher Keaton take the left fork and continue down to the T-junction, ignoring the public footpath sign on the left. Turn left on to the busy road, cross Keaton Bridge, and turn immediately left on to the public footpath marked Cole Lane, coast-to-coast Erme-Plym Trail. Now follow from ** below.*

For those on the longer route, carry on down the long hill into the village of Ermington; you emerge into the village "square" beside the pub, The Crooked Spire, named because of the church's twisted spire; it was put up with oak beams that weren't completely seasoned, and subsequently twisted as they dried. Unfortunately although the board outside the pub promises good food and accommodation you will not find either inside, but you can enjoy a pint of Doombar. The church is majestic inside, and boasts a holy well in the field to the south.

From the pub, bear left through the square, turn right opposite the war memorial, turn left opposite the school into Fawns Close, and right into the playing field. Follow the path straight across, climb the steps to the busy road, turn left, cross the bridge over the Erme, and turn immediately left towards Strode. You have rejoined the Erme-Plym Trail, which takes you the rest of the way.

Climb the long hill, beside the Ludbrook for the first 100m or so. Pass Ermecot House and Strode House. At the top of the hill ("Strode") is a gateway on the left. Step up to the gate for a view down the valley to Ermington. 30m further on take the (first) public footpath to the left over a stile, from where you can see across the valley the radio mast which you passed earlier. From here you can also see the hamlets of Higher Keaton across the valley, and Thornham down by the river. Keep down to the right-hand-side of this field to the gateway at the bottom; beware, this can become extremely muddy in wet weather.

The unusual stone stile is built on to a massive stone gatepost almost a metre square. These posts are common in this part of the country; presumably when they were built the landowners had a surplus of materials, labour and money.

Unusual stone stile

Over the stile, the direct path crosses the next field diagonally, past the telegraph pole in the middle, towards another unusual stone stile, just above two magnificent oak trees. However, you may wish to veer to the right, over what is probably a Neolithic long barrow, to look at the barn with the rusty roof. The near end wall, with the huge blocked window, dates to the 17thC, though most of it was built around 1760; the thatched roof was replaced with corrugated iron in the early 20thC. It's a threshing barn, or winnowing barn, with a big doorway on one

Threshing barn

side and a smaller one opposite to allow the wind to blow through and blow the chaff away from the ears of wheat, when the grain was tossed in a sieve.

The big settlement crack in the north-west end wall appears to have occurred soon after construction, and may have happened because that wall is built in the soft soil of the long barrow's ditch. Note the triangular owl hole high up in the south-east end wall; a resident owl would have been a valuable controller of mice. There is often an owl in residence, and there are cattle shelters with mangers (for cattle feed) in the sheds around the west corner.

Between the second unusual stile and the adjacent gateway is a curious structure known locally as the "bus stop", although no bus has ever been there. There were originally three wide seats, covered over, with lilac planted on the roof. During the 19thC Thornham was an important house, and this field, sometimes called the "tree field", may have been a pleasure ground or arboretum. Young gentlemen would escort their ladies over the bridge and up here to enjoy the view, especially in the evening sun.

From the bus stop, follow the obvious path diagonally down the field, noting the massive gateposts at the bottom, then across the right-hand side of two more fields to a third stile, this one of stone bricks, and on to a road. Turn left, down to a busy road in 150m. Turn left again, and

The bus stop

Stone-brick stile

200m later turn right, immediately before a small stone bridge, on to Cole Lane.

**This is where the long and short routes merge.*

The road passes Keaton Weir and becomes a path, which runs for 400m through trees beside the tranquil River Erme. You can sometimes see fish in the river during the summer months: sea trout and salmon go up river to spawn. Among the birds along the river are pied wagtails, dippers, kingfishers, ducks, herons, cormorants, and goosanders. Looking at this placid stream, it's hard to believe that after heavy rain on Dartmoor the

Kissing gate

An elephant's nest in a rhubarb tree

river becomes a raging torrent, which in 2012 seriously flooded several houses just downstream of the weir.

At the end of the wood is a kissing gate, and the path carries on along the side of the field ahead. Note 10m after the gate the curious tree on the right. It's a magnificent beech, but has an unusual thicket of shoots two or three metres off the ground. A lad who used to walk along here called it "an elephant's nest in a rhubarb tree".

This field can be wet and even boggy after a lot of rain. You may find it useful to veer left for 100m from the far end of the hedge to get around the worst patch. As you cross the field you have a splendid view of the newly restored Victorian mansion, Cleeve, which dominates the opposite hillside, surrounded by trees, and faces south down the valley.

Beside the next stile is a curious hut or byre, completely covered with ivy. It is built on a wall/hedge, and has gateways into both fields. Perhaps this was to help in moving a few selected cows from one field to the other. This is good territory for blackberries in the autumn. Walk along a farm track to the busy road. Bear left and follow the path beside the road until it dives through a hedge on to a football field. At the far end is the car park by the tennis club. You can keep to the right-hand side or cross the field and walk the last 200m beside the river.

Adam Hart-Davis *is a photographer, author, scientist and television presenter. Renowned for his presentation of 'Local Heroes', 'What the Romans Did for Us' and 'Tomorrow's World' he has also written many history and science books. His photographic work is second to none, see http://www.adam-hart-davis.org/photos.htm where you'll also glimpse his cats and chickens.*

Walk 8
Exploring Around the Dart
by Jan Barwick

Distance: 5 miles / 8km

Since moving here in 1972, I've constantly been beguiled by the Dart. In my opinion it truly is Britain's loveliest river. Spectacular views of this river are the hallmarks of this coastal walk from Dartmouth Castle, which takes in a short section of the South West Coast Path and a chunk of the Diamond Jubilee Way – a route created in 2012 to commemorate HM Queen Elizabeth's 60 years on the throne. It shows aspects of the river and Dartmouth itself only revealed to those prepared to venture off the beaten track and there is also plenty of countryside along the way for peaceful communing with nature. Although there are some climbs, it is not too strenuous and the footpaths, bridle paths and short sections of quiet country road make for easy walking.

Map: OS Explorer OL20 South Devon, Brixham to Newton Ferrers 1:25 000

Start point: Dartmouth Castle. Grid ref: SX886503. Postcode: TQ6 0JN

Directions to start: Dartmouth is in the South Hams, clearly signed on the A3122 and A379

Parking: Pay & display car park at Dartmouth Castle, and plenty of free parking in Castle Road itself

Public Transport: Dartmouth is well-served by buses, timetables at www.travelinesw.com. Alternatively travel by boat from Totnes or steam train to Kingswear followed by a ferry across the river (Dartmouth Steam Railway & Riverboat Company, 01803 555872). The nearest mainline railway is Paignton (5.8 miles)

Refreshments: Dartmouth Castle Tea Room, 01803 833897

Toilets: Near the Tea Room

Nearby places to stay: Bayards Cove Inn, 27 Lower Street, Dartmouth, 01803 839278; Charity House, Collaford Lane, Dartmouth, 01803 832176; The Victorian House, Vicarage Hill, Dartmouth, 01803 832766

Nearby places of interest: Coleton Fishacre Gardens (National Trust), near Kingswear, 01803 752466; Dartmouth Castle (English Heritage), 01803 833588

From Dartmouth Castle take the path and steps that lead uphill from the car park, then cross diagonally over the road at the top to the marked-off car parking spaces. At the right-hand end of these, take the footpath winding uphill into the woods to Gallant's Bower. At the first fork by the

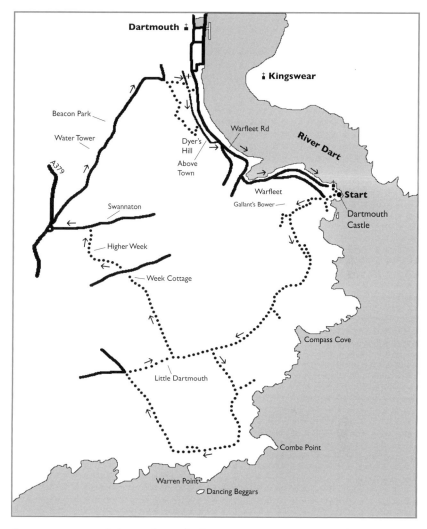

fingerpost, turn left, go through the gate and continue to the top. Here you can see the ancient remains of a Civil War defensive site and in spring the whole hilltop is awash with bluebells. Although the path curves round below the defences, it's worth climbing to the top to drink in the views across the river mouth and upstream towards Maypool. Return to the path which heads back into the woods and after a few hundred metres comes out in the road. Turn right uphill to the gate beyond the old coastguard cottages.

Above Willow Cove

You are now on a broad bridle track which curves around the head of the valley above Compass Cove to another gate. 500m beyond this you'll see a gateway and stile on your left.

Cross the stile and head downhill towards the coast to meet the South West Coast Path above Willow Cove, where you turn right and head westward. From your vantage point above these cliffs, you may spot the occasional seal, glimpse the diving flight of a peregrine falcon or hear the occasional punctuated rattle of the rare cirl bunting. Once beyond Combe Point various kind souls have donated seating and there are plenty of places to eat a picnic and gaze out over the sea in comfort. Above Warren

Point the path heads inland again and eventually emerges into the road at Little Dartmouth Car Park, where you meet the Diamond Jubilee Way.

Go right here, past the buildings of Little Dartmouth Farm, then just before the last building on the left, take the track signed to Week Cottage and follow until you hit the road at the bottom of the valley, where you turn left. Climb for 50m then turn sharp right up the track to Higher Week, pass above the

Gnarled tree above Willow Cove buildings and continue to Swannaton Road.

Another left-hand turn takes you up to the main road where you go right.

You now have a 20m stretch of main road (take great care) before forking right at the bend towards Jawbones. On the left at the bend near the water tower is Jawbones Beacon Park, a pleasant place to stop for a picnic, but the route continues downhill on the road, with views of the Dart gradually opening up.

When you reach a very sharp left-hand bend almost 700m from the water tower, turn right off the road into the field and follow the signed footpath

Kingswear from Jawbones

towards Dyer's Wood. Now you have the whole spread of Dartmouth and the estuary below you, about as good a view as it's possible to get, anywhere. Once in the wood, follow the path for about 150m. A fingerpost then directs you downhill to the left down steepish steps and into the road at Above Town. Notice the old water conduit, dated 1794, which supplied water to the houses in this part of the town in the days before piped water. Turn right here and continue along and then downhill to the junction, then right again into Warfleet Road. Just above Warfleet Creek take the left-hand turning into Castle Road, noticing the restored lime kilns above the creek on the left. When this branches, take the lower road and follow it back to your starting point at the Castle.

Dartmouth History
More than 600 years of defensive history is visible within a short distance of the Dart's mouth. In the 15th and 16th centuries, attacks by marauders from the sea were repelled by crossfire between the two castles of Dartmouth and Kingswear, and a chain that stretched across the river mouth could be lowered to keep out invaders. The castle supplanted an earlier 14th century structure, of which the remains can be seen above the car park, and which makes a suitably atmospheric backdrop to the town's open-air Shakespeare productions in August. On the hilltop above the castle are relics of Britain's only Civil War. The Royalist Garrison endured the bitter winter of 1656 in the redoubt at Gallant's Bower, only to fall to the Parliamentarians the following year. The Victorian gun battery, seaward of the tea rooms, replaced an earlier Tudor structure and continued in use through both World Wars.

Jan Barwick was Editor of Devon Life magazine until retirement in 2009. Since then she has continued freelance writing, albeit on a lesser scale, preferring to spend time trying to keep her garden under control, exploring the countryside on foot and involving herself in Dartmouth's thriving University of the Third Age.

Walk 9
Bantham, Thurlestone & the River Avon
by Jackie Humphries

Distance: 5 miles / 8km

This is a lovely figure of 8 walk which has a "bit of everything". You begin at the sandy, unspoilt beach at Bantham, with views across the bay to the famous art deco hotel on Burgh Island. Follow the coastal footpath to the village of Thurlestone, with its ancient church and 16thC Village Inn, before enjoying a riverside walk along the picturesque River Avon. The walk is moderate with one steep ascent and descent. It includes the coastal footpath, public footpaths through fields and woodland, farm track, surfaced road, stiles and steps.

Map: OS Explorer OL20 South Devon, Brixham to Newton Ferrers 1:25 000
Start point: Bantham Beach. Grid ref: SX664436. Postcode: TQ7 3AN
Directions to start: Bantham is situated in the South Hams about 5 miles west of Kingsbridge. It can be accessed off the A379/A381
Parking: Bantham Car Park
Public Transport: There is a limited bus service to this area, details available at www.travelinesw.com. The nearest railway station is Ivybridge (8.1miles)
Refreshments: Bantham Village Stores & Coffee Shop, 01548 560645; Sloop Inn, Bantham, 01548 560489; Village Inn, Thurlestone, 01548 563525
Toilets: Bantham Car Park
Nearby places to stay: Henley Hotel, Bigbury-on-Sea, 01548 810240; Sloop Inn, Bantham, 01548 560489; Thurlestone Hotel, Thurlestone, 01548 560382
Nearby places of interest: Burgh Island, accessed from Bigbury-on-Sea; South Devon Chilli Farm, Loddiswell, 01548 550782

From Bantham Car Park walk towards the lifeguard's hut on the left of the beach. Go through the kissing gate signed "Coastal Footpath Thurlestone 1 m". Follow the footpath up the steep hill, through the next kissing gate and continue uphill. At the bench sit and rest awhile whilst enjoying the panoramic views over Bigbury Bay. Continue walking uphill and go straight on at the information board.

You now have views along the next stretch of coast, towards Thurlestone Rock, Hope Cove and Bolt Tail in the distance. At the green hut above Broadsands Beach, turn left and follow the footpath and black and white

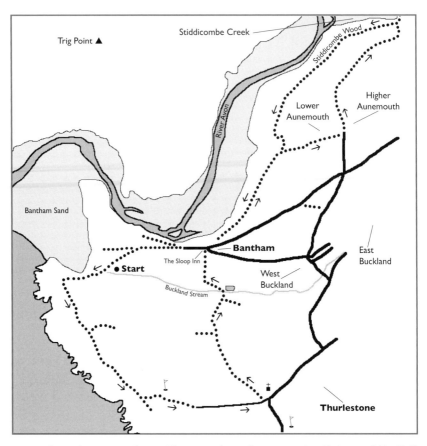

posts directly across the golf course (watching out for flying golf balls!) Continue straight ahead along Eddystone Road.

At the end of the road turn left on the lane just before All Saints' Church, Thurlestone, signed "Bantham ¾ m". Climb over the stone stile and follow the footpath through the fields, through the next gate and over the next stile. Continue straight ahead and downhill following the yellow waymarker. Before descending the steep hill stop and enjoy the stunning views over Bantham, the River Avon and Burgh Island. At the bottom of the hill follow the footpath through the gate then over two stiles. This field is often very muddy (even in summer) and it is best to keep to the edge of the field so walk towards the water trough and then turn left around it.

Go up the steps, through the gate and follow the footpath between hedges to the Sloop Inn at Bantham. You have now completed the first part of the figure of 8. Take the second road on the right, around the white clapperboard house, and walk uphill a short distance to the track on the left between two houses signed "Private Road. Private Access Only. Aveton Gifford 3½ m. Avon Estuary Walk". Follow the track alongside the estuary.

Go through the gate and continue to follow the track as it bends to the right. (Ignore the sign for the estuary walk going through a gap in the fence – you will come back that way.) Walk through the next gate and up the lane to the right of the farm.

At the junction turn left signed "public footpath" walking downhill between Higher Aunemouth and the farm gates. Follow the track until you reach three gates together situated on either side of the track and leading into fields. Continue downhill until you reach the next gate on the left. (The public footpath sign is on the right but hidden in the hedge.) Go through this gate and walk downhill heading for the right hand edge of the woods on Stiddicombe Creek.

Climb the stile into Stiddicombe Woods and follow the path through the woodland, abundant with wild garlic and bluebells in spring; you are now on the Avon Estuary Walk. At the junction bear left. When you exit

The Avon Estuary and Burgh Island

The River Avon & Bantham

The River Avon flows 22 miles from Dartmoor to the sea, with the last 4 miles cutting its way through a narrow, steep sided valley to Bigbury Bay. The Avon provides an important habitat for birds, including shag, fulmar, common sandpiper, little egret, little grebe, curlew, wigeon, oystercatcher, redshank  and greenshank. The inlet is a sea bass nursery and Atlantic salmon and sea trout spawn upriver.

Archaeological excavations suggest there was once a Romano-British settlement on the site of the car park and dunes of Bantham Ham. Artefacts from the 5th–7thC have been found, including pottery, bone tools, javelin heads, iron knives and fish hooks. It is thought the site may have been a temporary or seasonal settlement where goods and food were traded.

the woods continue straight ahead following the Avon Estuary Walk signs (a blue heron) along the top edge of the fields above the river. You now have glorious views as the river opens up below you and winds its way out to sea.

Go through a gate, fork right and immediately through another gate, continue to follow the estuary/blue heron signs. Cross the boardwalk

View from the coastal footpath

Hookney Tor (Walk 11)

Across the River Dart towards Kingswear Castle (Walk 8)

Butchers' Row, Barnstaple (Walk 5)

Looking along the Exmoor coastline (Walk 16)

Beside the River Otter (Walk 3)

View from the top of Yarde Down Lane (Walk 14)

Red Admiral (Walk 15)

Bantham Boathouse (Walk 9)

The ruined 'Pleasure House' with Stoke Church beyond (Walk 6)

Indulgencies! (Walk 16) *Dartmoor foal (Walk 2)*

Across the Culm Valley (Walk 12)

Grey seal (Walk 13)

View from Hartland Quay (Walk 6)

View from Raddon Hills (Walk 4)

Heading for Morte Point (Walk 13)

St. Peter's Church, Zeal Monachorum (Walk 10)

bridge over a small stream, climb a stile and then a few steps. Walk through the gap in the fence, turn right and you are back on the track to Bantham. From here retrace your steps back to the village.

At the main road turn right and walking past the Sloop Inn follow the road back to the car park. I would, however, recommend that you don't walk past the Sloop Inn and instead finish your walk with a refreshing drink!

Jackie Humphries' "Walk This Way" is a holiday company that has been developed with the purpose of making it easier for you to visit and discover the South Hams on foot. The walks are designed to take you  *through tiny hamlets, picturesque villages, market towns, bustling harbours and, of course, along the spectacular coastline. For more information please contact: Jackie Humphries – jackie@walk-this-way.co.uk, www.walk-this-way.co.uk*

Walk 10
Zeal Monachorum
by Tony Byrne

Distance: 2¼, 3 or 5¼ miles / 3.6, 5 or 8½km

This delightful walk, the length of which can be varied according to preference, encompasses the best that the inland countryside of Devon has to offer, from woodland to rivers, hidden pathways, extensive views and architectural interest. There are a few uphill and downhill stretches, but nothing very challenging.

Map: OS Explorer 113 Okehampton 1:25 000

Start point: By the main gate of St Peter's Church, in front of the clock tower and by the Jubilee Bench. Grid ref: SS720040. Postcode EX17 6DF

Directions to start: Zeal Monachorum is 18 miles north west of Exeter, between the A3072 (Copplestone to Bow) and B3220 (Morchard Road to Winkleigh)

Parking: On-street parking around the centre of the village (please exercise courtesy towards residents). The far side of the churchyard from our start point is usually convenient

Public Transport: Irregular service from Exeter with Carmel Coaches, timetable available at www.travelinesw.com. Nearest railway station is Morchard Road (2 miles)

Refreshments & Toilets: The Waie Inn, 01363 82348

Nearby places to stay: Nichols Nymet House, Nichols Nymet, 01837 82626; The Waie Inn, 01363 82348

Nearby places of interest: Finch Foundry (National Trust), Sticklepath, 01837 840046; Okehampton Castle (English Heritage), 01837 52844

The walk starts by the Jubilee bench, at the main gate to the church. Facing outwards, turn right and follow the lane, skirting the churchyard and passing the village hall. Beyond the National Speed Limit signs turn right onto a footpath. After 40m pass through a gateway on the left and go straight ahead through the field with the boundary to your right. On reaching the right-hand end of a farm building, pass through a gate, go through an opening in the back of the building and via another gate into the next small field. Follow the right edge of this, exiting via a gated enclosure, marked with an arrow. It can be muddy here. Descend via a fenced area through a small copse, with steps and boardwalk, soon

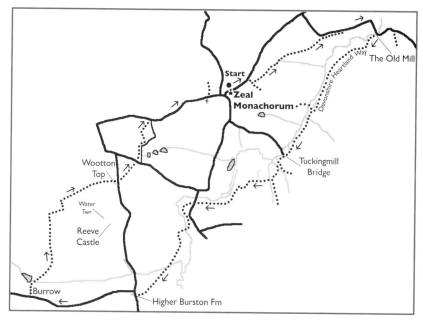

emerging over a stile. From here climb diagonally right through a field, up towards the end of the hedge boundary, which you follow, the hedge on your left.

At the end of this field, cross a stile into what was Down St Mary Vineyard, where we once had a wonderful view of a fox leaping to catch

Churchyard, Zeal Monachorum

an unsuspecting vole, oblivious to our presence. Follow the path above the former vineyard terraces, which at the time of writing had recently been replanted with young trees. There are good views of the river meandering below you here. Near the end of the terraces exit through a gateway on the left. Turn right along the lane. After a sharp right bend, go over a small bridge then turn right again by The Old Mill to follow a footpath through a gate between fences (towards woodland). Go through another gate at the end of the short track and follow the arrow to the right, passing through a gate into a field and following the right-hand boundary to a stile in the corner. Cross this, continuing in the same line, to reach another stile to the right of the woodland. This area is good for sightings of soaring buzzards, ravens and bullfinches.

Enter the woodland and follow the track for a few hundred metres, until it veers down to the right, towards an interesting wooden bridge over

Quarry machinery

the river. It is worth detouring onto this and enjoying the views along the water. However, your path exits left before you reach this, into a field, following the arrow straight ahead towards a metal gate on the far side. Pass through the gate, then bear left out of the trees into another field. Here turn right, guided by a post, following the boundary for 150m or so towards a rising area. At the foot of this, exit through a gate by an oak tree, joining a track.

You soon approach some large, decaying machinery, from when this was a working quarry. Although now somewhat decrepit, these possess a certain beauty. Continue ahead, leaving the quarry, emerging by the ancient Tuckingmill Bridge.

For the shortest route, turn right here and follow the lane to a T-junction, at which go right to return to the centre of Zeal Monachorum.

The longer routes continue ahead, on a public bridleway, shortly passing ruined mill buildings and the water wheel on the right. At the entrance

Tuckingmill Bridge

to cottage gardens, the footpath and bridleway signs direct you to the left. Follow this, but almost immediately fork right along the bridleway, rising gently between hedges to a wooden gate. Go through this and another gateway opposite, then turn right off the bridleway and onto the footpath. Follow the right-hand boundary of the field, pass through an opening in the hedge at the end and follow the same line through the next field. At the end of the field, turn left, climbing gently for about 80m to reach a gate recessed into the right boundary. Exit here onto a woodland path, bearing left, gently down through a small copse. Continue ahead on leaving the trees with woodland still to the left, a small field and stream to the right, fine views greeting you as you proceed. A well defined path leads ahead through the field to a metal gate in the far hedge, emerging onto a lane.

The second shorter route is to turn right here, over the bridge and then follow the lane back to Zeal Monachorum.

For the longest route cross the lane, joining the footpath opposite and bearing slightly left across the field. At the bottom of the field, take a clear path left into light woodland, following a stream on your right until, within 200m, the path veers right to a small wooden bridge over the stream. Cross this and go diagonally left through the field to meet a gate at the bottom of a hedge boundary. Pass through this, entering another field and follow the left boundary, which then swings right to a gateway. Leave this field, bearing slightly right through the next towards farm buildings and a gate in the hedge. Pass through two gates, and go slightly right uphill to a gateway onto the lane opposite Higher Burston Farmhouse. Bear slightly right, taking the lane towards North Tawton. Follow this for about ½ mile to Burrow, enjoying views ahead and left to Dartmoor. Just before reaching Burrow glance back to your right to see the splendid Reeve Castle, built by an eccentric Victorian for his young bride. The water tower behind the property is also visible.

Between the modern barns at Burrow and the cob wall by the farmhouse turn right along a bridleway, a pond soon being visible over a wall to your left. The path descends briefly and then rises, climbing between hedges. There are good views towards Bow to your right as you pass

Leaving the woodland

Zeal Monachorum

Zeal Monachorum, which means "The Cell of the Monks", was gifted to the Abbey of Buckfast by King Cnut in 1018 and remained in the ownership of the Abbey until the dissolution of the monasteries under Henry VIII in 1539. The monastic and ecclesiastical links can still be seen in many of the property names in the village. It is believed that the substantial yew tree in the churchyard is over 1000 years old.

gateways. At the top, reach a collection of gates. Go straight on through a gate with (part of) a blue bridleway arrow on it, keeping the hedge on your right. Stunning views of large flocks of starlings are often seen here, wheeling through the skies. The views behind are also spectacular. Pass the line of trees level with the water tower and, after 60m, pass through a gateway in the right-hand corner and turn right. Cross this field, passing a ruined barn and go through a gate in the opposite hedge. Turn left along the field boundary, swinging to the right at the end of the field and keeping the boundary on the left. Pass through several gates and field boundaries with views of Zeal Monachorum ahead, until reaching the farm buildings of Wootton Top.

View near end of walk

The working farmyard, through which you pass, can be rather mucky. Go through several gates, finally emerging onto the lane. Pass through the gate opposite into the field and bear slightly left towards the village. Emerge onto a small lane, cross it and join another footpath opposite. Follow this, towards farm buildings, the field boundary to your right. At the barns, exit through a gate on the right-hand side. Head towards a cob barn and just before it turn left, following the arrow between farm buildings, across a grassy area to a gate. Follow another arrow uphill to a metal gate and through this into a field. Ascend here, the hedge on your right. Pass through the next gate and veer diagonally right towards a gateway close to the opposite corner, taking time to look behind, at the wonderful patchwork fields stretching into the distance.

Exit via the gate onto the lane, turn right and follow this, passing some lovely cottages as you return to the village.

Tony Byrne is an experienced walker, runner and keen naturalist who, in addition to undertaking several long distance routes, including Hadrian's Wall and a substantial section of the Pennine Way, has enjoyed walking in the Devon countryside for over 30 years. Usually office-bound, he loves to get out into the fresh air during weekends and holidays and explore hidden parts of the county.

Walk 11
Bennett's Cross, Grimspound & Hookney Tor
by **Belinda Whitworth**

Distance: 4 miles / 6.5km

This walk introduces you not only to Dartmoor's space, silence and ocean-like views, but also to its prehistoric, medieval and industrial past. The route is not difficult but spotting paths can be tricky and they don't always conform to what is shown on the map, so a compass is helpful and, as ever on the moor, take clothing for all weathers.

Map: OS Explorer Outdoor Leisure 28 Dartmoor 1:25 000
Start point: Bennett's Cross. Grid ref: SX680816. Postcode (of inn, ½ mile south west of Bennett's Cross): PL20 6TA
Directions to start: Bennett's Cross is on the B3212 between Moretonhampstead and Postbridge
Parking: Bennett's Cross car parking area (SX679815)
Public Transport: Infrequent buses from Dartline Coaches run between Moretonhampstead and Postbridge, timetables at www.travelinesw.com. Nearest railway stations are Yeoford or Okehampton (both about 10 miles)
Refreshments: Warren House Inn, 01822 880208
Toilets: None en route
Nearby places to stay: Beechwood, Postbridge, 01822 880332; The Cherrybrook, Two Bridges, 01822 880260
Nearby places of interest: Dartmoor Prison Museum, Princetown, 01822 322130; Green Hill Arts Gallery & Heritage Centre, Moretonhampstead, 01647 440775
Note: Be aware: this route crosses open moorland, so a map, compass and clear conditions are necessary

Have a look at the cross before you start. About 6 feet high, it is one of 130 put up by medieval monks so that they could find their way over the moor. The crosses were also used as boundary markers and this one is inscribed WB, which stands for 'warren bounds'. (More about 'warrens' later.)

Back at the car park, take the broad grassy path at right angles to the road (ESE). After approximately 60 paces take a right fork, also broad and grassy, now heading roughly SSE as shown on the OS map.

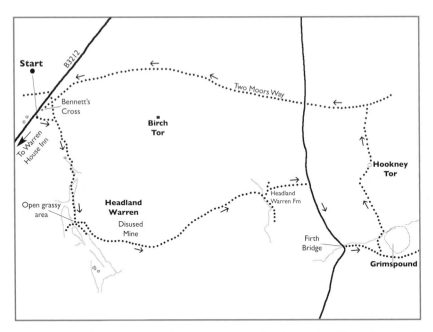

Soon you will find yourself in an area of hillocks and gullies, the result of tin-mining – which took place on the moor from the 12thC to the mid-20thC. You will also spot the remains of buildings as well as deep watery holes and shafts, so be careful. Ironically, this is the prettiest part of the walk with birds, sheep, wildflowers and trees all finding shelter here.

Medieval Bennett's Cross, one of over a hundred crosses
which helped monks find their way on the moor

*A contorted willow, its bark coated in lichen, moss and ferns,
profiting from a watery hollow and the shelter created by tin-mining*

It's hard to believe, but trees once covered most of the moor. Humans began to clear them in the Stone Age (around 5000 BCE), first to encourage deer and then for farming. Their primitive techniques (exhausting one area and then moving on), combined with a colder and wetter climate, left the impoverished soil and bare landscape that exists today.

After about ten minutes you will see some stone enclosures to your left and then the path is crossed by another, gravelly, path. Turn left (SE) on to the new path. This takes you to a lovely open grassy area with one of

The open grassy area with its stream and clapper bridge – and Ellie!

Dartmoor's sparkling streams, crossed by one of the moor's distinctive stone-slab or 'clapper' bridges. This area is a favourite with the moor's semi-wild ponies. These once helped work the mines and the farms but are now largely left to fend for themselves and have a hard time in cold winters.

Back on your path, cross the grassy area and then fork left (eastish) on to a grassy path which climbs gently uphill. To your left you will now see some stone piles and tumbledown mounds. These are the remains of 'pillow mounds', built for rabbits and hares which were kept on the moor for pelt and meat from the middle ages until the mid-20thC, and are part of the warren marked by the cross.

Past the drystone-walled enclosure (which you leave to your right) note more mining gullies on your right and to the left Birch Tor. Tor simply means hill, but on Dartmoor the word is used for the strange rocky outcrops on the tops of hills which look artificial but are in fact completely natural and the result of weathering.

Around now you might like to look back at the Warren House Inn in its lonely splendour. It is said to be the third highest pub in England and in the winter of 1963 was cut off by snow for nearly three months. Its fire has been alight since 1845.

The lonely Warren House Inn

Carry on climbing and away to your right on the side of a hill a prehistoric stone 'row' (actually, it's three) will appear. The moor's prehistoric heritage is outstanding – with stone rows, stone circles, single stones, burial mounds, chambered tombs and 'hut circles', to name just some of what you can find. What's more, you can wander right up to the remains – and touch them – and often you will have them to yourself. Unfortunately, it's not easy to scramble over to the stone row from this direction but soon you will be arriving at the moor's most impressive prehistoric site.

Sheltering on Hookney Tor

Straight ahead is Hookney Tor (which you will be climbing) and down to your right a farm. Descend to the farm, leaving it to your right, and head for the small road which you can see in front of you (various paths). At the road turn right.

Five minutes down the road, and just before it curves to the right, you will come across a layby on your right. Head up the slope to the left (various paths). Stone slabs will start to appear slightly to your right embedded in the ground, initially random and then marking a path. Follow them. (This path is a nineteenth-century restoration.)

After about ten minutes' climb in total the path brings you to the unmistakable outer walls of the Bronze Age settlement of Grimspound.

Grimspound from Hookney Tor

These were once 9 feet thick and at least 6 feet high. Inside are 24 stone (or 'hut') circles, the remains of dwellings. These would have been topped with a wooden lattice and turf.

Wander round, get a feel for the place, and then take the path just below the site that heads more or less north to Hookney Tor. (This too has been paved.)

On the tor take shelter from the moor's near-constant wind then at its highest (eastern) point follow a grassy path heading northish towards some drystone walls. To your right you will see a hump on the top of a hill. This is King's Barrow, a prehistoric burial mound. Look back and you will see that you have walked past a similar hump – another burial mound (labelled 'tumulus' on the OS map).

When you get to a ruined wall, go through the gap marked by two large stones and turn left (west) on to a grassy path. This is the Two Moors Way, a long-distance footpath that crosses both Exmoor and Dartmoor. Descend to the road, keeping the wall to your left and enjoying the moorscape.

Go straight over the road and follow the path as it continues on the other side (noting the peaty puddles created by multitudinous human feet).

You now have a trek of 15–20 minutes across featureless heather moorland. Eventually it will incline upwards and at the top of the slope you will see below you the car park where you left your car. Before hurrying gratefully down the path, rest awhile in the semi-circular stone shelter to your left.

Hut entrance, Grimspound

Belinda Whitworth has lived in rural Devon since 1978 and walks in it every day (if she can). Having worked as a book editor and non-fiction writer for twenty years, specialising in complementary health and the environment, she is now exploring fiction writing. See Belinda's blog 'Mad Englishwoman and Dog' (www.belinda-whitworth.blogspot.co.uk) for more.

Hemyock
by **Jo Shipton** (*photos* **Paul Adams**)

Distance: 5 miles / 8km

I have enjoyed many walks from Hemyock with its woodland, flowers, valleys and superb views; another reason why it's so pleasant to walk here is that you can often walk and meet no one else at all. It seems like an in-between kind of place which has a sense of permanence and self-containment. This walk goes through fields, lanes, tracks and valleys. There are some uphill stretches.

Map: OS Explorer 128 Taunton & Blackdown Hills 1:25 000
Start point: Outside the Blackdown Healthy Living Centre, Riverside/Lower Millhayes. Grid ref: ST140139. Postcode EX15 3SH
Directions to start: Hemyock is near the Devon/Somerset border, 5 miles south of Wellington
Parking: On road – please exercise courtesy
Public Transport: Hemyock is served by buses operated by Stagecoach South West and Redwoods Travel, details online at www.travelinesw.com. The nearest railway station is Tiverton Parkway (5.8 miles)
Refreshments: The Half Moon Inn, Clayhidon, 01823 680291
Toilets: None en route but there are public toilets next to the Parish Hall in Hemyock village centre
Nearby places to stay: Pounds, Hemyock, 01823 680802; Regency House, Hemyock, 01823 680238
Nearby places of interest: Coldharbour Mill, Uffculme, 01884 840960; Wellington Museum, Wellington, 07971 242904 (TIC 01823 663379); Wellington Monument (site always open, Monument undergoing restoration until at least 2015), grid ref: ST137172

From Riverside go left along Lower Millhayes and at the end of the 'industrial buildings' take the steps up to the right. Walk across the green past a small play area, turn left through the gate and walk in front of the cottages. After 1 Higher Millhayes, turn right into the start of a track.

Carry on up the track past 'Green Peace' and into the field following the hedge line on the right. Proceed through the next two fields, turning to stop and admire the view. Walk over a small footbridge and cross the stile into the next field. Then head up towards a stile which takes you onto

View over the Culm Valley from the Hemyock-Wellington Road

the Hemyock-Wellington road. Turn right – take care as this road can be busy.

After a short distance take the 'no through road' on the right, which is a small pleasant lane with wild flowers and views on the right-hand side, and continue on to Maidengreen House. After passing this on your right proceed straight ahead down the 'middle' track which soon becomes stony. When you reach the bottom you emerge onto a small road, turn left here towards Tanhouse Farm. Immediately after the farm turn right into another small road which winds up a hill; this is Black Lane.

Continue up Black Lane for ½ mile stopping to admire the view of Wellington Monument on your left. There is woodland to either side. As you reach the brow of the hill go through a wooden gate on your left which is signed as 'Clayhidon Turbary, Devon Wildlife Trust'. This would

be a pleasant place to stop for a picnic on a sunny day with good views of the Wellington Monument and far reaching views in either direction. It is an area of heathland and mire where parishioners were allowed to cut the peat for fuel – a practice known as 'turbary'. Continue along the path at the top of the turbary. At the end of the path turn right and go through the gate by an abandoned cottage. Walk straight up the field to the gate, go through and into the farmyard (Mount Pleasant Farm). Proceed through two further gates and out onto the track. At the end of the track cross the stile on the right of the gate onto the road. Turn left.

If you do not wish to go to The Half Moon Inn resume walk at (**) below.

Follow the road and very soon, after 10m, turn right over a cattle grid onto a trackway. Go straight ahead (with hilltop views of surrounding woodland) and when you reach the edge of a garden at a barn conversion the path turns to the right. Go through the gate and walk in front of the Old Rectory, then through another gate and turn right towards the road. This is Clayhidon and the Half Moon Inn is on your left. If the weather's fine it is a great place to have a drink (good local beer) and admire the view from the beer garden, down the valley towards Rosemary Lane and Hemyock.

After stopping at the pub, retrace your steps back to the road by the cattle grid where you need to turn right along the road with further views of the Wellington Monument.

(**) Continue on the road for 500m until you reach Jennings Farm on your left with an adjacent bridleway sign. Turn left, walk past the smallholding and proceed down the hill where the track goes through two gates, turning left and left again (bridleway sign). Continue along the track

Valley between Clayhidon and Hemyock

passing Knapp Cottage on your right then turn left through the next gate (beside farm buildings) continuing on the footpath to the next gate (way marked) and into a meadow with rushes and seasonal flowers. At the far end of the meadow turn right and walk across a footbridge over the stream then over a stile. Follow the line of the hedge on the right and go over the stile in the right-hand corner of the field, immediately turn left and continue along the trackway at the bottom of the field. Go through a gate and continue along the concrete track going through a further two gates and into the farmyard at Middle Ashculme Farm.

Walk through the farmyard then turn left on the road, walk down the hill passing Ashculme Cottage on your left. As you walk down the hill the

Trackway near Middle Ashculme Farm

road levels out and Tanhouse Farm is on the left (where you turned to start walking up Black Lane). Walk along the road, ignoring the next left turn 450m after Tanhouse Farm. Beyond this continue for about 40m on the road then turn right over a small footbridge and stile. Once in the field, cross diagonally and continue through a gap into the adjoining field, continuing diagonally across this field – please note that there are often cows grazing here. In the far corner of the field, beside a farm building, there is a stile; once over this you are beside Byes Farm. Turn right along the road passing Deepsellick Farm on your right returning towards Lower Millhayes, the Healthy Living Centre and your start point.

> *Some of my earliest memories of walking are when my mother and I would walk along roads near our village; she grew up on a farm and told me the names of the wild flowers we saw on our walks. Thanks to her, this engendered a lifetime love of walking and interest in nature. I regularly walk with friends, belong to the Ramblers' Association and also lead walks for various local walking groups.*
> *For details of walks in your area please visit: www.ramblers.co.uk/walksfinder*

Mortehoe & Lee
by **Simone Stanbrook-Byrne**

Distance: 7¼ miles / 11½km

A superb walk encompassing some of the best coastal scenery on offer, verdant woodland, delightful villages and an excellent dog-friendly pub en route. The area is brilliant for bird watching – you have the chance of seeing peregrine, the fastest creatures on earth when they stoop. You may also see seals and possibly dolphins. Inevitably the walk involves some steep ups and downs but it really is worth the effort.

Map: Outdoor Leisure 139: Bideford, Ilfracombe & Barnstaple 1:25 000
Start point: Mortehoe Car Park. Grid ref: SS457452. Postcode: EX34 7DT
Directions to start: Mortehoe is 6 miles west of Ilfracombe and 1¼ miles north of Woolacombe
Parking: Mortehoe Car Park
Public Transport: The number 31 and 303 buses pass through Mortehoe and both are operated by Filers Travel. Timetables available online at www.travelinesw.com. Nearest railway station is Barnstaple (10 miles)
Refreshments: Chichester Arms, Mortehoe, 01271 870411; Grampus Inn, Lee, 01271 862906; Rockleigh House, The Square, Mortehoe, 01271 870704
Toilets: In Mortehoe Car Park and in Lee
Nearby places to stay: Rockleigh House, The Square, Mortehoe, 01271 870704; Shaftsboro Farm, Lee, 01271 865029
Nearby places of interest: Chambercombe Manor, Chambercombe Lane, Ilfracombe, 01271 862624; Mortehoe Museum, 01271 870028
Note: Be aware: part of the route is across open moorland, so a map is very useful and clear conditions necessary

---

From the car park turn left along the lane through the village, towards the parish church. Just before the church, as the road swings left, go right up the lane towards the village hall and cemetery, passing the church on your left and heading for the coast path. Keep straight ahead when you reach the cemetery, following a dirt track to pass through gates. This is Morte Point Memorial Park and is all access land. You will see an information board about the area not far from the gates. Near here you

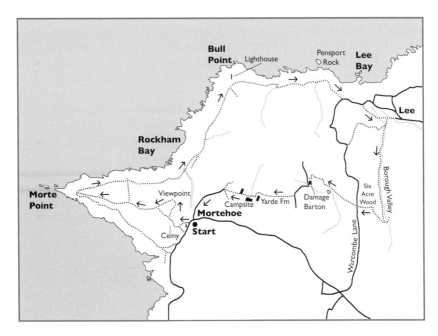

will also find a wooden fingerpost pointing you uphill to an elevated viewpoint.

Head for this viewpoint, winding your way up in the direction of the pointer to the top of the hill, about 300m away from the information board. The paths are well-trodden although there are only occasional arrows, but keep heading up until you find the site of the former lookout which was built at the start of WWI but demolished in 1932. The spot was well-chosen as the views are superb and the men who kept watch are commemorated on one of the plaques here: John Dyer, Thomas Parker and Samuel Yeo. Morte Point juts out into the sea to the west, north east of it along the coast is the lighthouse at Bull Point and looking south is the vast expanse of Morte Bay and Woolacombe Beach.

From here you can see the path out to the end of Morte Point. Descend from the lookout and walk west towards the Point, a fabulous stretch of walking which abounds with enticing paths – relish it. The route of the walk heads west, dropping down towards the sea until, just above the end of the headland, you meet a clear, hard-trodden, earth crossing path, the South West Coast Path. At this point it is also the Tarka Trail, a long distance route crossing the countryside celebrated in Henry Williamson's book *Tarka the Otter*. Turn right on the coast path, the Atlantic to your left. You now follow the coast path, passing Rockham Bay, all the way to the lighthouse at Bull Point, just under 2 rugged miles away. Ignore any footpaths heading inland back to Mortehoe, unless you're tiring and want an escape route – you will see the village outskirts as you continue. When you reach Bull Point Lighthouse look for the three-way fingerpost and continue on the coast path to Lee, 1½ miles away. Eventually you reach a footbridge spanning a stream – enjoy the lovely seaward view then keep going. It was near here that we had a good view of peregrine on the cliffs. The coast path crosses a second footbridge some way on and when you reach a three-way fingerpost denoting 'steep path to sandy cove' to the left, ignore it unless you wish to explore. Your way continues up steps on the coast path above Lee Bay. This area is called Damage Cliffs. The path reaches a lane on the outskirts of Lee, turn left down it and follow it for about 300m as it swings right past the large gates of Lee Manor. A little way beyond here you find a right turn with a multiple-fingered post set against the wall. Leave the coast path, going right along this lane signed for the car park, toilets and footpath to Lee village.

Pass the car park on your left, followed by the public toilets. The tarmac lane becomes a stony path, keep ahead to reach a footpath fingerpost on

Hazy view to Woolacombe beach

the right. This is your way but first I suggest you keep ahead into the village for a short detour to The Grampus Inn and a look round this attractive area, before returning to this fingerpost.

Back at the fingerpost cross the stile and walk through the field with the wall on your left. At the end of the field cross another stile followed by a footbridge into woodland with a nearby three-way fingerpost. Your route follows the path beside the stream through the refreshing, sylvan area of Borough Valley. In just over ½ mile you reach a crossing path. When we were here a three-way fingerpost leant drunkenly against the bank. Left goes down to a footbridge but the way you want is, I'm afraid, steeply uphill through the trees on the path to Damage Barton. Emerge from the

Rugged coastal scenery

woodland and cross the stile a short distance away, walking through the field beyond in the direction of the yellow arrow. You reach a lane, cross over to a high stile on the far side. The post adjacent to this high stile was pointing in a rather misleading direction. From the stile look diagonally right across the field to glimpse another fingerpost in the distance, beyond the field corner and set high up. Follow this line to a gate set back in the corner and beyond this bear right up the bank to the elevated fingerpost.

From here the route varies slightly to what is shown on the OS map. Take the right hand option from the post which points across the field to an obvious gate in the far right hand boundary. When you get there you may spot a well-engorsed fingerpost to the right of the gate – it's hard to see

Bull Point Lighthouse and Trinity House

The original Bull Point Lighthouse was built in
1879 after many ships succumbed off the
coast here. In 1972 the headland subsided
rendering some of the buildings unsafe. For
two years Trinity House used an old
lighthouse tower, imported from Braunton,
while another lighthouse was constructed
further back from the cliff edge. Equipment from the old lighthouse was
put to use in the new one. The foghorn ceased its call in 1988 and the
lighthouse is now fully automated, its associated buildings finding a new
lease of life as holiday cottages.

The corporation of Trinity House, whose remit is to aid the safety of
shipping and seafarers, is a charity that received a Royal Charter from
Henry VIII in 1514. This was granted to a fraternity of seafarers called The
Guild of the Holy Trinity who regulated the pilotage of shipping in waters
frequented by the King. Trinity House is best known for its administration
of the lighthouse system of England, Wales, the Channel Islands and
Gibraltar but also provides other aids to navigation such as lightships, buoys
and satellite navigation. It also licences and supplies Deep Sea Pilots who
assist ships with navigation, and another, less familiar aspect of its work is
the provision of retirement homes for ex-mariners.

Lee Bay

it without lacerating your face. From the gate follow the track through the field – the track is sometimes clear, sometimes indistinct. You may notice a pond beyond the fence to the left if you veer over. Keep going on the track as it winds between gorse bushes. You reach a two-way fingerpost 250m from the gate, which has both pointers going back! Keep ahead here to a yellow-topped post within 100m.

At this post go almost 90° left to descend past a few trees and gorse bushes to a well-concealed gate about 100m from the post. Through the gate you'll find another yellow-arrow directing you down to quickly meet a clear path along which you turn right. You are now approaching the farm buildings of Damage Barton. Within 50m you reach a clear track and a two-way fingerpost. Go left down the track and at the buildings turn right, still on the track with the wall of an old stone barn on your left. At the end of the wall you enter a yard area, bear diagonally left across the yard and you'll see a clear sign pointing you towards Mortehoe.

Follow this direction, passing the attractive house on your left and walking along the drive past a pond – an area beautiful with snowdrops in the early part of the year. Keep going up the drive, passing occasional

The coast path   *Walking through Borough Valley*

benches, until, about 250m from the house, you find a footpath going right as the drive bends left. The yellow arrow points you through the field with the boundary to the right. At the end of the field you find two gateways. Go through the one on the left, continuing with the boundary still on your right. This rises to another gate, beyond which keep going in the same direction, boundary to your right.

At the end of the field cross the stile and descend the path beyond, down steps, to arrive at Yarde Farm. A two way fingerpost directs you ahead on the track to reach a three-way fingerpost in about 50m. Go through the gateway, walking diagonally left through the field, still towards Mortehoe. This brings you to the far bottom corner of the field. Go through a gate then follow the path past a pond. The path winds between buildings, follow the arrows to arrive at the business area of a camping and caravanning site. Keep ahead past the various facilities and away from the buildings, following the drive in a westerly direction to reach gates, emerging from the site onto a lane. Go left on the lane and follow it for about 0.3 mile, back to the centre of the village and the car park from which you started.

Simone Stanbrook-Byrne wrote her first guide for Mid Devon in 2000. In 2010 she teamed up with James Clancy to form Culm Valley Publishing which specialises in outdoor leisure guides for the West Country. Together they produce an expanding series of books for the region: www.culmvalleypublishing.co.uk

Walk 14
Bradninch
by **Sue Jackson**

Distance: 4½ miles / 7.25km

This Mid Devon walk gives far reaching views of the Exe Estuary and the Blackdown Hills from the highest points, in addition to a glimpse of the area's industrial heritage in the shape of the paper mills at Hele and Silverton. The route comprises quiet rural lanes, tracks and fields – where it could be muddy in places if the weather has been wet. Always best to come prepared! It is occasionally steep but the resulting views are superb.

Map: OS Explorer 115 Exmouth & Sidmouth and OS Explorer 114 Exeter & the Exe Valley 1:25 000

Start point: Hornbeam Gardens Car Park, Bradninch. Grid ref: ST001041. Postcode: EX5 4NZ

Directions to start: Bradninch lies to the south of Cullompton (off M5 at Junction 28) and can be accessed from the B3181

Parking: Hornbeam Gardens Car Park or in a suitable on road parking space – please exercise courtesy

Public Transport: Regular buses from Exeter and Cullompton, timetable available at www.travelinesw.com. Nearest railway station is Whimple (5 miles)

Refreshments: Castle Inn, Bradninch, 01392 881378; White Lion, Bradninch, 01392 881263

Toilets: None en route

Nearby places to stay: Heath Gardens, Broadclyst, 01392 462311; Silverton Inn, Silverton, 01392 860196; Three Tuns, Silverton, 01392 860352

Nearby places of interest: Charwell Wetlands Nature Reserve, Bradninch, grid ref: SS997036 (off Hele Road near junction with Charwell Meadow)

Leave the car park and turn left onto Parsonage Street to make your way onto Fore Street, turning left to walk up towards the centre of the town. You will notice 'Comfort House' across the road, a master weaver's house built in 1681, which is the only thatched property remaining in Fore Street. As you continue up the road you will pass Church Street which leads to St Disen's, a mid 15thC church which possesses a notable painted screen. There is a plaque on the gates to the churchyard dedicated to the American pioneer Daniel Boone's father who was baptised in the church.

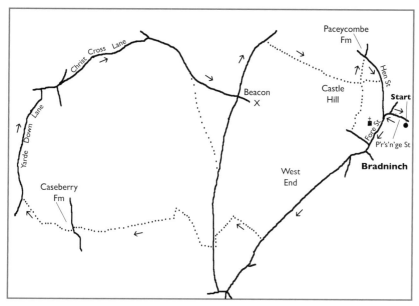

You will come up past the Castle Hotel and next door you will find the town's Guildhall which is used for council meetings and many local group activities including the well established Bradninch Music Festival held annually in June. Continue straight down the hill, past the White Lion Inn and along West End Road until reaching a footpath just past Passmore Road and opposite Asher House.

Take the footpath and follow it around the field until you come to a metal gate to exit the field. Cross the lane and enter another field walking straight across to a metal gate. Go through and turn right down a grassy track. Another metal gate leads you into a field which you cross bearing slightly left to the lane ahead. (If it has been wet, this field can be a bit boggy so keep a watch on where you are treading.) Turn left onto the lane and you will soon see a footpath on the right up a few steps. Do make sure that you use the footpath and do not continue along the lane. Once in the field, follow the line of telegraph poles ahead until you see the gateway into the next field. The route continues straight across this field to the next gate but, if crops are being grown, please keep to the left edge of this and the next field. You will come to a lane with a cottage (Caseberry Cottage) just before it. Turn left out of the field and then right

Looking down towards Caseberry and the Culm Valley

up the drive (there is a Columbpark Limousin cattle sign) to Caseberry Farm. Keep straight on past some outbuildings and between the house and farmyard to a metal gate with a green disc showing the footpath. This leads you into a steep field. It may be easiest to walk up the left edge of this field unless you enjoy vertical walking! Once you reach the metal gate at the top, go through and bear right diagonally up to another metal gate onto the lane. Do always ensure that gates are properly closed to keep any grazing livestock in their fields. This is now a great spot to turn around and take in the panoramic views of the Exe Estuary and the Haldon Hills above it – and a possible picnic lunch stop.

Extensive views to the Sidmouth Gap

Views to Killerton and beyond from Yarde Down Lane

Turn right along the lane (Yarde Down Lane) and follow this up to the T-junction. Depending on the time of year you may see a variety of flowers and birdlife along the lane. There are often buzzards gliding and soaring over the surrounding fields in search of prey. Another common sight is a buzzard being swooped upon by a crow.

Turn right at the T-junction (you will now be on Christ Cross Lane) and look out for the views in either direction – if the hedgerows are not too tall you will see the Blackdown Hills to your left. Stay on this lane for about a mile, passing a sign showing one mile to Bradninch, until you reach the crossroads at Beacon Cross. It is worth another stop here to look through the gateway on the right; the estuary in the distance again, with

View from Beacon Cross

the paper mill at Hele in the foreground; traffic on the motorway (feeling glad that you are not amongst it), possibly a train travelling between Exeter and Tiverton Parkway; Hembury Hill Fort ahead slightly to the left and the Blackdown Hills round to the left.

Turn left at Beacon Cross and follow the lane until you come to a pair of field gates on the right, taking the second gateway where the footpath is signed. Keep to the hedge line and after almost ½ mile you will come to a footpath crossroads. (To the right is Castle Hill where there was a wooden fortress back in the 7thC.) Take the left path across the field and continue to a stile in the hedge. Take care on the steps on the other side as they are quite narrow. You will come out onto the lane just below Paceycombe Farm. Turn right down Hen (meaning 'old') Street noting how many properties have 'fowl' connotations! At the bottom of the hill turn left and immediately right onto Parsonage Street to return to Hornbeam Gardens Car Park.

Sue Jackson is an enthusiastic walker and often leads walks for the Exeter and District group of the Ramblers' Association, having joined them in 2000 after moving house to a new area. It has proved to be a wonderful way to discover and enjoy the Mid Devon countryside and especially rewarding to lead other walkers on paths that they may previously never have trodden. For details of walks in your area please visit: http://www.ramblers.co.uk/walksfinder

Kingston, Wonwell & the Erme Estuary
by Jackie Humphries

Distance: 5¾ miles / 9.25km

This is a strenuous walk with panoramic views in all directions. There are two quiet, unspoilt beaches, Westcombe and Wonwell, where you can rest and paddle, although it would be better to wait until you reach Wonwell Beach on the Erme estuary as the majority of the hard walking is then behind you. The route includes coastal and public footpaths through fields and woodland, bridleways, country lanes, stiles and steps. As there are no refreshment stops during this walk please make sure you have enough to eat and drink, the steep hills make for thirsty work!

Map: OS Explorer OL20 South Devon, Brixham to Newton Ferrers 1:25 000
Start point: St. James' Church. Grid ref: SX635477. Postcode TQ7 4QB
Directions to start: Kingston is in the South Hams about 14 miles east of Plymouth. It can be accessed off the A379
Parking: On-street by St. James' Church (please exercise courtesy)
Public Transport: Limited buses, details from www.travelinesw.com. The nearest railway station is Ivybridge (5.5 miles)
Refreshments: Dolphin Inn, Kingston, 01548 810314
Toilets: None en route
Nearby places to stay: Dolphin Inn, Kingston, 01548 810314; Ringmore Vean, Ringmore, 01548 810382; Windwood Farm, Ringmore, 01548 810615
Nearby places of interest: South Devon Chilli Farm, Loddiswell, 01548 810314

From the church walk past the Dolphin Inn, turn right at the T-junction then take the 1st lane on the left. Follow the lane straight ahead as it becomes a public bridleway. Continue on this for 1 mile until you reach a gate signed "Public Footpath Westcombe Beach ½ m" follow the footpath along the valley until you reach the beach and coastal footpath.

Turn right going through the gate and climb the very steep hill directly in front of you. This is Hoist Point, so called because seaweed used to be hauled up from the beach to fertilize the potato crop. Whilst getting your breath back at the top, views can be enjoyed over Burgh Island, Bigbury Bay and Bolt Tail.

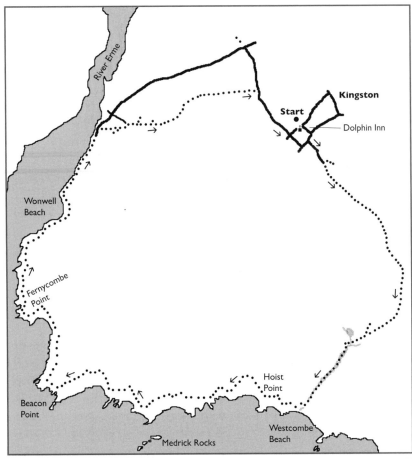

The Erme estuary at low tide

Continue to follow the coastal footpath over Beacon Point; you now have wonderful panoramic views west along the coast to Stoke Point. Many of the cliffs along this part of the coast were used for the lighting of beacons, Beacon Point being the first to warn of the approach of the Spanish Armada in the 16thC. As you round Fernycombe Point the wide sands of the Erme Estuary are displayed below.

The path makes its way between bushes and shrubs, over a small stream and emerges at the beautiful Wonwell Beach. This is a quiet and unspoilt place in which to stop, rest and watch the waves. Dogs and horses can often be seen enjoying their exercise on the beach and in the surf.

Heading down the valley towards Westcombe Beach

If the tide is out walk along the beach to the old slipway and follow it up to the lane. If the tide is in, return to the footpath and follow it above the beach, then go down a few steps to the lane.

Walk up the lane for about 75m then turn right into the woods signed "Public Footpath Kingston 1¼ m". Follow the footpath uphill through the woodland. When you emerge from the woods climb the stile, you now have views over rolling countryside towards Dartmoor. Go over the next stile and follow the footpath along the top of the field, proceed through the gate following the path between hedges, over another stile and then diagonally across the field.

The Erme Estuary

Many birds can be seen on this walk, particularly in the Erme estuary. These include redshank, dunlin, oystercatcher, curlew, turnstone, little egret (inset) and, of course, gulls. On the cliffs at either side of the beach, birds such as stonechat, pipit, whitethroat and linnet can be found. At migration times rarer  visitors have been seen, including osprey, hoopoe, and golden oriole. Whilst walking along the cliffs of Beacon Point look out for peregrine falcon.

The coastline here is lined with rocks, stacks and tiny islands, the most lethal being Mary's Rocks, hidden beneath the water at the mouth of the Erme estuary. Fourteen shipwrecks lie on the seabed, the oldest being a Bronze Age vessel used in the local tin trade. Ingots of tin have been found on the wreck, most likely to have been mined on Dartmoor and possibly en route to Burgh Island, a prehistoric tin trading centre.

Continue on the footpath until you reach the road. Turn right on the road and head back towards the village. At the crossroads turn left and then turn right at the church to return to where you began the walk.

The cliffs at Westcombe Beach

Time for a rest and to admire the view!

Jackie Humphries' "*Walk This Way*" *is a holiday company that has been developed with the purpose of making it easier for you to visit and discover the South Hams on foot. The walks are designed to take you*  *through tiny hamlets, picturesque villages, market towns, bustling harbours and, of course, along the spectacular coastline. For more information please contact: Jackie Humphries – jackie@walk-this-way.co.uk, www.walk-this-way.co.uk*

Walk 16

Little Switzerland
by **James Clancy**

Distance: 5, 7½ or 8¼ miles / 8, 12 or 13.3km

This beautiful route, through an area dubbed Little Switzerland, encompasses stunning river gorges, an iron age hillfort, spectacular coastal scenery and the curious natural phenomena to be found in the Valley of Rocks. There are some steepish ascents and good footwear is essential especially after wet weather.

Map: OS Outdoor Leisure 9, Exmoor 1:25 000

Start point: The Esplanade Car Park, Lynmouth. Grid ref SS719498. Postcode: EX35 6EQ

Directions to start: Lynmouth is situated on the northern edge of Exmoor on the north coast. It can be accessed via the A39

Parking: Lynmouth offers numerous places to park. Try the Esplanade Car Park, where, for a reasonably modest sum, you can park all day

Public transport: Lynmouth is served by buses run by Filers Travel and Quantock Motor Services. Timetables available online at www.travelinesw.com. The nearest railway station is Barnstaple (15 miles)

Refreshments: Watersmeet (NT) is a must (opening times can vary out of season, it's worth checking before you go), 01598 753348. Mother Meldrum's in the Valley of Rocks shouldn't be missed either, 01598 753667. Hewitt's is recommended for cream teas on the way back, 01598 752293

Toilets: These are well-signposted in Lynton and Lynmouth and can also be found at Watersmeet and the Valley of Rocks

Nearby places to stay: Heatherville Hotel, Tors Park, Lynmouth, 01598 752327; Lorna Doone House, 4 Tors Rd, Lynmouth, 01598 753354; Rock House Hotel, Lynmouth, 01598 753508

Nearby places of interest: Exmoor Coast Boat Trips, 01598 753207. Glen Lyn Gorge, Lynmouth, 01598 753207. Lyn Model Railway, Watersmeet Road, Lynmouth, 01598 753330. Lynmouth Flood Memorial Hall (next to harbour)

Leave the Esplanade Car Park and head along the road into Lynmouth. Ahead of you, across the bay, you can see Foreland Point and Countisbury Hill with its transmission mast. Pass the funicular Cliff Railway on your right, unique in that it is the only one in the world powered entirely by water. Bear right with the road as it goes past the 14thC Rising Sun Inn and shortly after this the Bath Hotel, entering the rather quaint shopping precinct. Emerge from here and proceed along

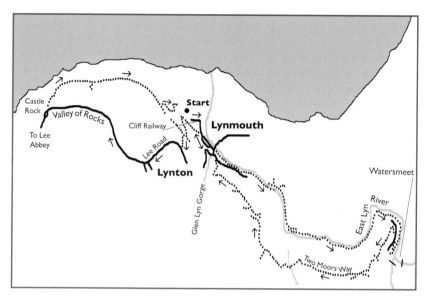

Riverside Road to a T-junction. Cross the road (with caution) and descend steps to walk along a stone-walled path beside a car park. The East Lyn River is on your left. Keep along this path. On the far bank of the river you can see Glenville House, Lorna Doone House and some attractive stone cottages. Don't cross the river here but as you continue do spare a glance back towards Lynmouth as the view behind is as picturesque as the one in front.

Soon you reach Middleham Memorial Gardens, the site of the cottages destroyed in the 1952 flood (see page 109). Visit these via the flight of steps at the far end.

Leave Middleham and continue in the same direction along the river. Cross at the next bridge, signposted for Watersmeet, and continue with the river to your right. This is one of our favourite stretches, it becomes very dramatic after heavy rain. After several hundred metres the path ascends. Go with it, admiring views of the river in the gorge below, until you reach a right fork signposted 'Watersmeet Riverside Walk'. Take this and head back down, crossing another bridge and continuing with the river on your left. Keep on this path, passing without crossing another bridge, after which look out for the site of the former Lynrock Mineral

Waterfall near Watersmeet

Water Factory, whose buildings were destroyed in the flood. Near here you can see an old fireplace and one of the company's ginger beer bottles set into the wall of the gorge.

You pass the fenced garden of Myrtleberry. Keep ahead on the footpath with the fence on your left. Soon the river opens up slightly, keep following it. It's worth noticing the amazing plant habitats in the gorge walls through which you're passing. There is an area here for picnics and options on paths, but they all merge in a few metres to continue with the river to your left. Don't be tempted to cross the next bridge, other than to admire the view from the middle. Soon you see the welcome sight of Watersmeet House where there have been tea gardens since Edwardian times. As the path forks follow the rustic post fence down to the left, crossing first Hoaroak Water and then the East Lyn River – the two waters which meet here. Refresh yourself with tea before continuing.

Leave the tea gardens, re-crossing the two bridges and bearing right after the second bridge. Zigzag up the path leaving the gorge and your route into Watersmeet behind you. At the third bend is a sign 'Lynbridge via The Cleaves'. Follow this up to the lane, it emerges at the staff parking area. Cross the road and pick up the path opposite signposted 'Lynton and Lynmouth via The Cleaves', following this up through the trees. This will lead you to Myrtleberry North, Iron Age Enclosure. Walk across this hillfort to the steps which you can see leading up the hillside ahead of you. Yes, I'm afraid so: these are calling you to climb them. There are glorious views as you approach the steps, look right to see Lynton nestling in the surrounding hills.

At the top of the steps keep ahead until the path is joined from the left by the Two Moors Way (denoted by M above W). Bear right here, towards

Lynton and Lynmouth, along a lovely path. There is a steep wooded hanger to your right, rising hillside to your left and eventually the view opens up to the bay with, on a clear day, Wales in the distance across the Bristol Channel. From here you can look down to Lynmouth and your starting point.

The path passes through two footpath gates, still signposted for Lynton and Lynmouth. Look across to the opposite hillside, you will have a good view of Countisbury Hill and The Blue Ball Inn – an excellent hostelry for another time. This path eventually winds downwards to reach a small stony footbridge, then continues up again affording glorious sea views

Lynmouth Harbour

to help you on your way as you climb. Once you're high enough look back along the deeply wooded gorge through which you walked earlier, with farmland rising above it. The view makes the climb very worthwhile.

Eventually you reach a three-way fingerpost, at which point head right downhill on the grassy path towards Lynmouth. This is still the Two Moors Way and zigzags all the way back down to the village, dropping steadily through woodland. Keep downhill on the main path, ignoring any side turns. Nearing Lynmouth you reach a sign welcoming you to the northern end of the Two Moors Way. As you descend you pass some attractive cottages before reaching Watersmeet Road. Here turn left passing Shelley's Hotel. Keep left along the road to admire the view up the Glen Lyn Gorge from the bridge. Now cross the road on the bridge and go down a tarmac path between stone walls. Down here on the left you will see a plaque noting the flood height on 15 August 1952 (see page 109).

Retrace your steps through Lynmouth to the Cliff Railway. Those not wishing to take this have the option of using the footpath to ascend to Lynton. This starts just a few metres before the entrance to the railway, and is a very steep climb. For those taking the railway there is a small fare for humans and dogs but the experience is well worth it. Savour it.

Emerging from the railway in Lynton walk ahead on the tarmac road to the main shopping street through the town. This is Lee Road, turn right when you join it, soon passing the grand Town Hall and later a rather arresting graveyard flanked by some amazing cedar trees. You are heading towards the Valley of Rocks.

Less than a mile from Lynton the road leads into the valley which abounds with semi-wild goats and Exmoor ponies – all part of the natural management of this spectacular area. On your right you will see what is probably one of the most scenic cricket pitches in England. Ahead of you is the towering mass of Castle Rock. Just after the cricket pitch is Mother Meldrum's Tea Rooms and Gardens. This is another must.

When you feel able to extract yourself from Mother Meldrum's continue along the road towards Castle Rock. Here you have an option.

Those wishing to extend the walk through the valley can do so by following the road across the small roundabout and continuing. This will soon lead you past the fingerpost pointing right to draw your attention to The White Lady. Admire her, then continue if you wish to Lee Abbey, a church retreat and holiday centre. This is about ¾ mile beyond Castle Rock. When you have explored as far as you wish, return to Castle Rock, which the energetic can climb to discover some stunning views. Mother Meldrum's Cave is another point of interest, signposted up the hill on the opposite side of the road.

When you've had your fill of this area, return to Castle Rock and pick up the tarmac coast path past the telescope (the business end was missing when I was last there). Follow the path back along the cliffs, heading east towards Lynton & Lynmouth, sea to your left. Pause occasionally and glance behind you for one of the most dramatic views in Devon. Continue east on the path as it winds its way back. This is a glorious stretch of coastline, abundant with wild flowers, seabirds, roaming goats and possibly seals. You are being watched by the lighthouse in the distance ahead of you on Foreland Point. This was established in 1900 but automated in 1994. The original keeper's cottage can now be rented for holidays.

Eventually you reach a tree-covered stretch and pass through a gate. Just after the gate leave the main path and go left down a stony path through the trees. This is signed 'Lynmouth ½ mile'. Follow this as it zigzags down. This can be quite rough underfoot. Part way down this path you will come upon an enticing sign on a gate inviting you to partake of a legendary cream tea at Hewitt's. This is highly recommended and the views from here along the Exmoor coastline are simply stunning. Hewitt's is open 12–5 daily, but best to check if visiting out of season.

This path descends right into the Esplanade Car Park from whence you started.

The magnificent Valley of Rocks

Castle Rock and the White Lady

The Lynmouth Flood of 1952

Flood marker – Lynmouth

Extremes of weather and climate change are frequent features of 21stC news, but the picturesque village of Lynmouth was devastated by one such phenomenon some decades ago. In August 1952, after 9" (23cm) of rain fell in 24 hours, the already swollen rivers of the East and West Lyn were unable to cope with the deluge. Lynmouth and its environs bore the full force of millions of tonnes of water and its accompanying debris, resulting in the collapse of 39 buildings and the deaths of 34 people. Much speculation remains as to the cause of such excessive rainfall. Nowadays a tranquil garden marks the site of destroyed houses but it's sobering to consider the forces of nature which have shaped this landscape over the centuries.

James Clancy has co-authored 9 walking books with Simone Stanbrook-Byrne. Together they founded Culm Valley Publishing, which specialises in walking guides for the South West (www.culmvalleypublishing.co.uk). James has always enjoyed exploring this region and capturing the variety of scenery on offer with his trusty Canon EOS camera.

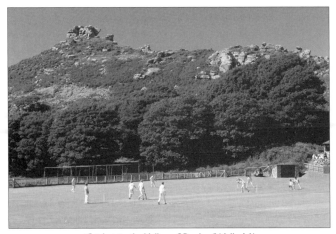

Cricket in the Valley of Rocks (Walk 16)

Coastpath sign near Blackpool Mill (Walk 6)

Misty landscape (Walk 14)

Hookney Tor (Walk 11)

Other guides from Culm Valley Publishing

The 'Circular Walks' series all contain fifteen walks through the magnificent countryside and coastal terrain of Devon.

Circular Walks in North Devon: including Exmoor
ISBN: 978-1-907942-09-9 **£6.99**

Circular Walks in Central Devon: the walking guide to Mid Devon
ISBN: 978-1-907942-01-3 **£6.99**

Circular Walks in East Devon
ISBN: 978-1-907942-08-2 **£6.99**

Circular Walks in the South Hams
ISBN: 978-1-907942-11-2 **£6.99**

The Dozen Dramatic series takes you to the most spectacular scenery each county has to offer. All walks are circular.

A Dozen Dramatic Walks in Devon
ISBN: 978-1-907942-00-6 **£5.99**

A Dozen Dramatic Walks in Cornwall
ISBN: 978-1-907942-03-7 **£5.99**

A Dozen Dramatic Walks in Somerset
ISBN: 978-1-907942-02-0 **£5.99**

A Dozen Dramatic Walks in Dorset
ISBN: 978-1-907942-04-4 **£5.99**

Shortish, circular walks exploring the history (and tea shops!) of Devon and Cornwall's fascinating towns.

Town Walks in Devon
ISBN: 978-1-907942-05-1 **£7.99**

Town Walks in Cornwall
ISBN: 978-1-907942-06-8 **£6.99**

All books available from Culm Valley Publishing: 01884 849085
www.culmvalleypublishing.co.uk / info@culmvalleypublishing.co.uk